"Bailey offers readers a profound gift. With clarity and skill, he introduces us to the dynamic ways theology and culture intersect. Culture, he insists, is a sacred space in which Christians make meaning, steward power, behold beauty, engage neighbors, and encounter the living God. Rejecting simplistic and reductionistic Christian understandings of culture, Bailey's newest work introduces us to the complex field of human action and divine grace that we call 'culture.'"

—**Matthew Kaemingk**, Richard John Mouw Institute of Faith and Public Life, Fuller Theological Seminary

"Reading *Interpreting Your World* was a lot like listening to a new album from one of my favorite bands. As I moved through the chapters, I encountered the kind of theological music I would love to make myself, if only I had half the imagination or skill. Equal parts innovative, surprising, and enlightening, this book sings. It should be required reading for any person of faith who is asking how to engage culture in more robust and life-giving ways—which is to say, everyone should read this book. I cannot recommend it highly enough."

—**Kutter Callaway**, Fuller Theological Seminary; coauthor of *Theology for Psychology and Counseling*

INTERPRETING
YOUR WORLD

INTERPRETING
YOUR WORLD

Five Lenses for Engaging
Theology and Culture

Justin Ariel Bailey

Foreword by Kevin J. Vanhoozer

B

Baker Academic

a division of Baker Publishing Group
Grand Rapids, Michigan

Published by Baker Academic
a division of Baker Publishing Group
PO Box 6287, Grand Rapids, MI 49516-6287
www.bakeracademic.com

Printed in the United States of America

Library of Congress Cataloging-in-Publication Data
Names: Bailey, Justin Ariel, 1981– author.
Title: Interpreting your world : five lenses for engaging theology and culture / Justin Ariel Bailey.
Description: Grand Rapids, Michigan : Baker Academic, a division of Baker Publishing Group, 2022. | Includes bibliographical references and index.
Identifiers: LCCN 2022006129 | ISBN 9781540965066 (paperback) | ISBN 9781540966056 (casebound) | ISBN 9781493437832 (pdf) | ISBN 9781493437825 (ebook)
Subjects: LCSH: Christianity and culture. | Christian philosophy.
Classification: LCC BR115.C8 B3335 2022 | DDC 261—dc23/eng/20220315
LC record available at https://lccn.loc.gov/2022006129

22   23   24   25   26   27   28   7   6   5   4   3   2   1

To Joshua David Beckett
"The name of one friend is better
than all the muses."

CONTENTS

FOREWORD

Why should theology, the science of God and of the sacred page, consort with something as "secular" as contemporary culture? And why should seminarians, prospective pastors and preachers, or for that matter, everyday Christians spend time learning how to interpret popular culture and critical race theory in addition to the Bible? Biblical interpretation we know, but who, cultural interpretation, are you, and why have you come to church?

In the 1980s, when I began my seminary teaching, few people talked about culture, and when it was mentioned, it was always *foreign*: something *they* had, over *there*. Much has changed since then. However, if anyone still questions the need for theology to engage culture, let them ponder Jesus's words: "Why do you see the speck that is in your brother's eye, but do not notice the log that is in your own eye?" (Matt. 7:3 ESV). The truth is that we are all creatures of culture, people who form and have been formed by (mentally, morally, even spiritually) everything in the world that is not a product of nature.

I introduced Justin Ariel Bailey to cultural hermeneutics almost twenty years ago. (You can read his account of this experience in the introduction.) I am happy to acknowledge that thanks to the present book, the student has now surpassed his teacher. I talked in class about the importance of giving thick descriptions of cultural objects and practices, but I am now learning from Justin how better to do this, thanks to his penta-focal glasses (the five lenses) that enable him to give even thicker descriptions of the cultural world, of the dialogue between theology and culture, than the ones I presented in class.

Yet why bother interpreting the world if, as Karl Marx stated, the point is to change it? This is a fair question. Many Christians want to transform culture by proclaiming the gospel, but this requires discernment. The title of John Stott's book on the topic accurately describes the challenge of preaching: *Between Two Worlds*. To be sure, a pastor is first and foremost a minister of God's Word, yet in order to bring the Word to bear upon the world, preachers need to know something about the people to whom and the contexts in which they are ministering. Knowing culture matters because culture, like religion, is in the business of shaping hearts: appealing to the imagination's need for meaningful stories and creating and satisfying desires.

Culture invariably informs our lived theology or, as Justin puts it in this book, "our sense of what is most real and what really matters." I sincerely believe that culture is the most powerful means of spiritual formation on earth—apart from the Holy Spirit, that is. Culture forms even the way we think about and read the Bible, which raises the question, Who is interpreting whom? It so happens that both the Bible and contemporary culture offer interpretations of our world, of everything that matters to us.

To preach or communicate the Word of God effectively in the present world, then, pastors need to know something about the biblical text *and* our contemporary context. To become what Jesus calls "fishers" of human beings (Matt. 4:19)—the kind of disciples who can make other disciples—it helps to know something about the water in which they live and move and have their being. For example, do they live in salt water or fresh water?

Justin offers five lenses on culture, five perspectives on the water in which we human-fish live and swim and have our being. The five lenses allow us not simply to stay on the surface of the water but to plumb its depths. Justin gives us tools to help us understand *why* people speak, act, and live as they do. And though he has moved beyond the culture as a meaningful text model, his book still contributes to the important goal of cultural literacy. For it is only when we are able to make sense of culture, and to understand its nature, function, and power, that we can begin to engage it theologically. The purpose of engaging culture is to gain cultural literacy, a prerequisite for cultural agency: the ability to make a difference, to inhabit one's culture in ways that befit followers of the Way of Jesus Christ. What is at stake in the dialogue between theology and culture that Justin here engages is nothing less than the shape of our discipleship.

If we rename Justin's first lens (the meaning dimension) the *semantic* dimension, then his five dimensions (semantic, power, ethical, religious, aesthetic) give rise to a handy mnemonic, the acronym SPERA, from the Latin for "hope." That is only fitting, for his overall approach to the relation of theology and culture is not replacement but fulfillment. The conversation between theology and culture that Justin conducts is not a zero-sum game with one winner and one loser. It is rather the warp and woof of the Christian life, and a must for every Christian who is serious about doing everything—especially eating and drinking at the table, in conversation with others—to the glory of God.

Kevin J. Vanhoozer
Research Professor of Systematic Theology
Trinity Evangelical Divinity School

ACKNOWLEDGMENTS

I once imagined writing to be a solitary project: a person alone with a pen and pad or laptop computer. And although writing is often lonely, no one can write alone. This book would not exist without the communities that have loved, nurtured, and upheld its writer. This includes my parents, Warren and Nathania Bailey, my sisters Jennifer and Jacquelyn, and many spiritual brothers and sisters, aunties and uncles, mentors and friends who have accompanied me on the way. My children, Benjamin and Sophia, have been my favorite teachers, reminding me of the joy of doing things "just for the heaven of it." And Melissa is the love of my life, reminding me that we are secure only because of the faithful love of another.

I owe special thanks to the many friends who cheered for the project, reviewed the proposal, read early drafts, and talked me through the tensions, including Bill Dyrness, Matthew Kaemingk, Cory Willson, Jeff Ploegstra, Joel Kok, Matthew Beimers, Davey Henreckson, Dave Mulder, David Moser, David Westfall, Gayle Doornbos, Jeremy Perigo, and Jay Shim. Laremy and company at The Fruited Plain Cafe kept me well caffeinated as I wrote, and the group known as the Dordtlings kept me sane.

I am grateful to John Hwang, whose vision to help academics with their "distribution problem," has given me a clearer focus for my public scholarship and service. The Kielstra Center at Dordt University provided me with time, space, and support to read, write, and rewrite, and the classroom at Dordt has been a wonderful place of inspiration and experimentation, especially the two courses I taught on Christianity and culture in 2021. Many thanks to the students in these courses for allowing me to "try out" my ideas and for being willing to "try on" the method in this book. Rylan Brue was a stellar research assistant who not only worked painstakingly through the endnotes and bibliographic material but also helped me frame the argument with scholarly sources, literary connections, and poetic language.

Thanks to Bob Hosack for believing in this project, to Jennifer Koenes for her editorial insight and direction, and to the whole team at Baker Academic for guiding it across the finish line. I was delighted when Kevin Vanhoozer agreed to write the foreword, which carries his characteristic wisdom and wit. Kevin introduced me to the theological interpretation of culture nearly two decades ago, and he continues to embody the interpretive virtues to which I continue to aspire.

I've dedicated the book to my dear friend Joshua Beckett, who for years has read almost every word I've written. When writing is lonely, or when I feel like an imposter, such a friend is better than any muse. His fierce fidelity has shaped my work, and my life, in so many ways.

I have always loved theology because it is an integrative discipline, because of the way it seeks to reflect on all of life before the face of God. So here I am, out of my depths, dabbling in disciplines that are worthy of a lifetime of attention. I pray I have done them some justice and that the good Lord would take up this offering of words and establish the work of my hands.

INTRODUCTION

Is There Anything to Say?

In the early aughts, I was working as a youth pastor in a small church on the north side of Chicago. The whole group could fit in one fifteen-passenger van, and yet it was quite diverse. My students were mostly non-white, ethnically Filipino, Puerto Rican, and Indian Americans. Some attended Chicago Public Schools, others were at private evangelical schools in the suburbs, still others went to private Catholic institutions. Led by me, a Filipino American raised in suburban Kansas City and educated in a predominantly white public school, one dynamic was always present: the complexity of culture.

I was raised in an independent Baptist church with a strong sense of countercultural purpose. If we used the word "culture," we prefaced it with a definite article: the culture. The culture was broadly synonymous with "the world," which was one part of the unholy trio—the world, the flesh, and the devil—with which we were at war. This youth group, however, defied such easy categorization. Rather than being the product of a definite monoculture (the culture), this youth group testified to a diverse mingling of ethnic and educational cultures.

But there was also another distinct world that the students shared: popular culture. Given the group's diversity, I began to see pop culture as common ground on which I could build. Developing pop culture literacy became a ministerial necessity as I worked to connect with the students. So

1

I took up breakdancing (I was not very good), listened to their music (the emo rock band Dashboard Confessional stands out in my memory), and joined them online in the emerging (pre-Facebook) social media world. I also endeavored to include pop culture references in my teaching. My analysis was clumsy, of the compare-and-contrast variety (this is what the culture says; this is what the Bible says). Most of the time, my forays into pop culture were met with embarrassed silence. If my critiques altered my students' habits of consumption, they rarely let me know.

An exception to this stands out. One student, upon giving his life to Christ, informed me that he wanted to destroy all his "secular" CDs. I am not sure where he got this idea, but it was not that surprising. There is a well-attested tradition of evangelicals destroying their "devil music," after the pattern of converted sorcerers who burned their magic books in the early church (Acts 19:19). When I was in high school, a Pentecostal friend of mine shattered his CDs using a sliding glass door. I had never advocated for such an act of cultural iconoclasm. But when my youth group student shared with me his desire to make a decisive break with his "past," I wanted to honor that desire. So I drove him to a bridge and watched him fling his rap and R&B CDs into the river below. Even then, I remember feeling conflicted about the action, for reasons beyond the act of littering we had just committed. I was happy that he wanted to follow the Lord. But did discipleship mean the *replacement* of everything he had previously loved? Is that how Christians are meant to relate to culture?

*   *   *   *   *

These questions still drive me, now two decades later. I find myself leading Christian college students in conversations about the relationship between faith and culture. In one class, I begin with a two-minute writing exercise using the following prompt: "What do you believe, and what difference does it make in your life?" Student responses to this question are occasionally provocative, but largely predictable. I have also consistently found something that fascinates me. Although students can speak eloquently about music, entertainment, sports, and politics, when it comes to matters of faith—their theology—many of them have difficulty articulating either the substance or the significance of their beliefs.

I do not share this to belittle my students, who have taught me so much. I share it to note the surplus of time, energy, and attention they have for discussing *culture*, especially when compared with their deficit of language for describing their *faith*. When reading through student responses to this question, I sometimes recall a summary statement from researchers who spent seven years studying the religious lives of American teenagers: "I believe there is a God and stuff."[1]

Perhaps it is not fair to expect fluency from my students when it comes to describing their faith. Vagueness hardly afflicts only the young and the restless. All of us know more, believe more, and sense more than we can say. Faith is a framework of meaning before it is a collection of discrete, easy-to-articulate beliefs. Even when we begin to speak, we find that our words fail us. We have a *felt* sense of the way the world is, which we are only sometimes able to describe clearly and coherently.

Our inability to describe our beliefs also reflects a coyness in our culture toward God-talk. The first time I met one of my neighbors, he learned that I taught theology at the local university. That's all I had to say before he interrupted: "I don't really know too much about religion and all that." I can certainly respect his reticence to speak about controversial topics, particularly with a "specialist." But I, who think and speak about theology for a living, share something of his shyness. Most of us do, for multiple reasons. The sheer diversity of religious perspectives in our culture makes faith feel fragile. In our polarized times, we don't want to offend anyone unnecessarily. And how can we know for sure that *our* religious vision gets reality right?

Some, like my neighbor, may respect theology but file it alongside other arcane disciplines, like theoretical physics. Still others feel more agnostic. God may be there, a metaphysical reality along with other unseen forces. But as long as you are kind to others and don't hurt anyone, do specific ideas about God really make a difference? This attitude is expressed a bit more eloquently by the poet A. C. Swinburne:

> From too much love of living,
>   From hope and fear set free,
> We thank with brief thanksgiving
>   Whatever gods may be.[2]

Our religious uncertainty breeds indifference, or at least indecision. Like the poet, we may be willing to tip our hats to a higher power, but we are less willing to reorient our lives in response to "whatever gods may be." It seems safer to think of God generically, to take a more laid-back approach: "I believe there is a God and stuff."

And yet.

And yet, like my students, we feel deeply and can speak lucidly about any number of topics that we care about: whether the Chicago Bears should replace their quarterback, whether the latest Christopher Nolan film was any good, or why the other political party is ruining the country. Religious questions remain; we still yearn for identity, seek relational connection, and strive for some purpose larger than ourselves. But now, pop culture is the primary space where these questions are publicly explored. We believe there is a God and stuff, and while the "stuff" of theology feels vaguely irrelevant, we are quite content with allowing the "stuff" of culture to be spelled out in staggering detail.

Perhaps younger generations simply lack the sophistication or the desire to mask what really matters to them. And regardless of how they were raised, theology doesn't really seem like it matters that much. What matters is figuring out who you are (identity), where you fit (belonging), and what you are supposed to do (purpose). Whom can I trust? When things are bad, can I expect tomorrow to be better? To what will I give my life? These questions, of course, all point to topics about which theology has much to say: faith, hope, and love (1 Cor. 13:13). And yet even those who self-identify as "religious" don't seem all that interested in theology's contribution to the questions that matter most (to say nothing of the irreligious).

Nevertheless, these conversations continue, and pop culture visionaries often have the loudest voices. To return to my class prompt: after asking the initial question about what they believe, I ask students to share a piece of popular culture that has been meaningful, that has changed their mind about something important, or that has brought relief in a time of difficulty. At first, students express themselves cautiously, expecting to be judged for their entertainment choices. But once they feel that their favorite bits of culture will be treated charitably, they begin to speak glowingly about the ways pop culture helps them cope, the ways it creates connections with friends and family, and the ways it offers them stories to make sense of a confusing world.[3]

It is this last part that consistently impresses me: the way that bits of culture offer unexpected anchors of meaning, identity, and belonging. One student identifies characters from her favorite shows as her "friends." Another student struggles to pass his classes but could tell you every first-round draft pick in the NBA lottery for the last thirty years. Others boast near-encyclopedic knowledge of various fantasy universes (whether manga, Marvel, or Middle-earth). Popular musicians are their poets, offering mantras in which they live and move and have their being. Whole worlds of meaning exist that matter so much to them, yet they do not expect their spiritual mentors to share space within these worlds, much less appreciation.

But the truth is that all of us are deeply shaped by our culture's conversations about the things that matter most. It is likely that when it comes to our working theology—broadly, our sense of what is most real and what really matters—we get more of it from culture than from Scripture or church tradition. Perhaps this is not surprising. Culture is all-encompassing, and it reaches us before theology does. Yet the goal of every follower of Christ is to reorient our lives in response to God's self-revelation. We want to allow the God who raised Jesus from the dead, who brought Israel out of Egypt, whose voice we hear in Holy Scripture, to reshape our sense of what is most real and what really matters, and with it the way we live in the world.

Who Speaks First? Getting a Grip on the Conversation

This is a noble goal: discipling our cultural imagination. But it is easier said than done. When my student threw his CDs into the river, and when I dissected Dashboard Confessional lyrics for my embarrassed youth group, we were both attempting cultural discipleship. Although my method was a bit more sophisticated, it basically amounted to the same thing: rejection and replacement. Indeed, many similar approaches to "cultural engagement" assume that the conversation between culture and theology is relatively straightforward. We compare what culture "says" with what theology "says" and proceed based on theology's superior perspective. In this picture, culture's contribution is only valuable insofar as it supplies the *wrong* answer, to be contrasted with or corrected by theology.

But there are problems with such a simplistic approach. To continue with the metaphor, a conversation between two or more parties is always more than the exchange of information. The *content* of a conversation (what is said) is embedded in a *context* (how it is said) and is energized by our sense of *connection* to our conversation partners (who is speaking). Let us take these in reverse order.

Connection. Communicators work hard to create a connection with their listeners. They do this because they know that our sense of *who* is speaking situates the way we process what is said. If I am criticized or praised, it will make a difference whether the words come from my wife, my father, a student, or a stranger. Similarly, a conversation with someone I want to impress—say, someone with the power to fire me—will proceed differently than a conversation where there is little "skin in the game." To put it plainly, when desire is engaged, the conversation matters more. When we treat ideas as though they are processed on a flat plane rather than through the filter of desire, we miss why cultural narratives captivate us. Most people think of theology as primarily a matter of the head. But we all feel instinctively that culture is a matter of the heart. It aims at our imagination. It plays to our hopes and our fears. It awakens our loves, identifies our anxieties, and names our intuitions. When culture "speaks," we encounter something to which we are deeply connected. It is not just a voice from "out there" but one that resonates with the voice "in here," representative of cultural stories that we have internalized and made our own.

Context. When it comes to communication, how you say it is as important as what you say. There is a difference between getting the message "I love you" via text, by owl, or in person. The method of delivery is full of meaning, and the way content is communicated—verbally or virtually, for example—shapes the communication, regardless of what the communicator wants to say.[4] Both culture and theology do more than "say"; that is, they do more than make assertions or state propositions. They comfort and console; they charm and convince. The voices speaking for either side come to us in forms that shape us; their force is felt, and their effects are evident long before we can extract any content. When culture speaks, it is doing more than just expressing ideas; it is impressing on us a way of being in the world ("This is the way"). We can resist the way; we can even subvert it. But we cannot easily ignore it.

Content. The full content of a conversation, embedded as it is in context and connection, can be difficult to discern. But it is even more difficult when multiple voices are speaking, especially if they are speaking at the same time, and at different volumes. The content of the conversation between theology and culture is difficult to discern because neither speaks in a single, unambiguous voice. Scripture is multivocal in its unity, requiring attentive literacy; traditions of biblical interpretation are deep and wide. In culture there can be a cacophony of voices. Some are loud; others are subtle. Some are constructive; others are critical. Some have large platforms and wield significant power. Some are distinguished by their dissent. They do not always agree among themselves. These voices are in conversation with each other, not just the person who is trying to listen in.

This complexity can become incredibly confusing, and so, living well begins with listening well. To borrow an image from Proverbs, many voices cry out to those who pass by: "Let all who are simple come to my house!" (Prov. 9:4). But as the Wisdom books show, rightly discerning between the voices requires us to become a particular kind of person. The challenge of discipleship is not just to distinguish who is speaking, what is being said, and how it matters. It is to contribute to the cultural conversation in ways that connect with those we are called to love and that cohere with God's redemptive vision for creation.

We are on God's stage, answerable for the lines we speak and the lives we lead. We may be tempted to recite familiar formulas, either from culture or from theology. But recitation rarely results in an illuminating exchange. What the world needs are faithful and creative conversationalists, rooted in the wisdom of theology yet hospitable to the wisdom of culture, wherever it is found.[5] For if we know that we are safe, "hidden with Christ in God" (Col. 3:3), we can engage the complexity of the conversation without fear.

Who Is Speaking? Distinguishing the Partners

It may be helpful to situate these two conversation partners with reference to a third party: religion. Indeed, much of the academic discussion takes religion rather than theology as culture's preferred partner.[6] Part of this preference is due to the desire to make descriptive rather than normative claims, to name *what is* rather than judging *what should be*. Thus, the academic study of religion has tended to narrow its focus to the human side of things. Its interest is in the social construction of religious meaning, in what can be accounted for without needing to invoke transcendent reality (like the existence of divine beings).[7] This does not exclude the possibility that there are real presences to which religion is responding. But religious studies as a discipline is methodologically agnostic. It wants to describe religious features regardless of whether a group's religious claims are true. Thus, religion is usually characterized in terms of rituals, beliefs, and sensibilities that capture a community's "reflections on the struggles of life."[8]

I will return to this method of investigation in chapter 4: religion and culture as ways of coping with matters of life and death. But I raise the religious studies perspective here to distinguish it from the project that I am pursuing. My primary interest remains in the dialogue between culture and theology. Theology—at least Christian theology—begins with revelation. It acknowledges as its fundamental principle a transcendent reality, one that is personal and accessible, supremely because God speaks. As the writer of Hebrews reminds us, "God spoke to our ancestors through the prophets at many times and in various ways, but in these last days he has spoken to us by his Son" (Heb. 1:1–2). Theology represents the effort to discern the divine voice and to answer back appropriately, in speech and action. It seeks to respond to a voice that comes to us from the outside, "good news from a far country" (Prov. 25:25 ESV), a message that we could not have discovered on our own, one that is genuinely, transformatively new.

Nevertheless, this word also makes itself intelligible for every new audience it encounters. Jesus's kingdom is "not of this world," and yet every time he describes it, he explains it in terms that are already familiar to his audience. The kingdom of God is like a mustard seed, like yeast, like a treasure hidden in a field. Theology responds to a voice that comes from the "outside," but it must always be expressed in terms that make sense on the "inside." This creates a tension: we feel, on the one hand, the claim of the gospel to distinguish ourselves from surrounding society. If Jesus is Lord, then we are called to create a biblically informed counterculture. But although the gospel brings a new creation (2 Cor. 5:17), this does not erase our prior context: our geographical location, our relational networks, our ethnic history. We are invited to respond to the gospel with respect to this particular cultural setting, allowing the leaven of the gospel to work its way through our world. The struggle to resolve the tension between these two poles—what missiologist Andrew Walls called the "pilgrim principle" and the "indigenizing principle"—has resulted in a "wild profusion" of diversity in expressions of Christian faith across time and space.[9]

All of this is to say that although the claim of the gospel is clear—that the world belongs to God, its Creator, Redeemer, and Renewer—our efforts to work this out in various cultural contexts can go astray. Cultural theology is slippery, both because theology is always already entangled in culture and because we are always in danger of domesticating God as a local deity. We are prone to overidentify cultural forms with authentic faith, assuming that our own forms are faithful and that all other forms are flawed. This is called "syncretism," and it is always easier to see in someone else's faith than in our own. And yet theology still must proceed, on the conviction that God speaks and that grounded in Scripture, guided by the Spirit, and in conversation with global Christianity[10] we can respond to the claims God makes on our cultural life.

How Shall We Proceed? Distinguishing Prepositions

Having set these terms, what will it take to become more skillful participants in the conversation between theology and culture? Let us distinguish possible directions in terms of three prepositions: "of," "from," and "for." We might engage in theology *of* culture, seeking to justify, orient, or evaluate our culture making in light of the biblical account of reality. Alternatively, we might listen for theology *from* culture, seeking to identify, discern, and resist the implicit theological visions that emerge from cultural artifacts. Finally, we might leverage theology *for* culture, drawing from theological resources to create, cultivate, and care for the communities in which we have been placed. The categories are far from clean, but we might say that "theology of" sees culture as a *work* we do, "theology from" sees culture as a *world* we discern, and "theology for" takes culture as a *web* we weave, one we share with significant others.

Culture as work: theology of *culture.* Up until this point, I have been speaking about culture as if all my readers know exactly what I mean. Yet defining culture is nearly impossible, not least because of how all-encompassing it seems. Consider the following definition from Clive

Marsh: "In its most general sense, it means the whole web of interpretive strategies by which human beings make sense of their experience. . . . Culture is thus a complex field of enquiry, because it potentially includes all forms of human creativity—whether consciously meaning-making or not: art, music, TV, film, poetry, fiction, drama, sculpture, sport, religion, gambling."[11] All forms of human creativity? That creates quite a range of subjects for us to theologize about! Where do we begin?

Here some historical context may help. The concept of culture emerged as a way of speaking about the refinement of the human spirit. The idea was that just as we can cultivate nature, we can also cultivate ourselves to be more attuned to the things that make life worth living, especially literature, art, and music. Just as extensive and enduring cultures can become civilizations,[12] humans can become civilized, elevated to a higher plane. The problem with this definition was that it too often assumed a hierarchy in which Europe was considered the pinnacle of what it meant to be refined. This recognition led to a more "modern" conception of culture, distinguishing *cultures* in the plural and treating them as separate but equal. This proved, however, to be incoherent (because it assumes a view from nowhere), impotent (because relativism cannot condemn unethical practices, like slavery), and illusory (because cultures rarely have clear external boundaries or broad internal consensus).[13]

The failure of the modern conception of culture, however, should not keep us from treating culture as a meaningful category. But it does complexify culture: it requires us to remember that culture is messy and that cultural meanings are contested from without and within. We can still acknowledge that there is *something* called culture, *something* that cultivates us, even if it is a *something* held together less by common concepts than by common concerns (e.g., what does it mean to be a good citizen, a good Christian, a good human?).

Another way of saying this is that culture is a *verb*, something we can't not do, part and parcel of being human. Culture, in the biblical story, represents the creative human vocation to unfold creation's intricacies and to image God in bringing order to chaos.[14] Culture making is an act of obedience to the divine mandate to take the good start given to us and to make it even better (Gen. 1:26–28). As the human response to God's creative action, our investment in culture is a deeply theological project. It may suppress or deny awareness of God (Rom. 1:18), but it cannot ignore the mandate to make something of the world.[15] The messiness of culture is, in many ways, a beautiful mess. It is a testimony to God's love of diversity and "manyness."[16] To engage in theology *of* culture is to evaluate our cultural activity (culture as work) in light of the theological vision we find in Scripture and traditions of interpretation. These sources do not "hover above" culture. God's revelatory action accommodates human culture, elevating it as a vehicle for revelation, without thereby canonizing its cultural forms.[17] One reason why theological reflection must be renewed in every generation is because the church seeks to discern God's will for the concrete time and place in which it finds itself. This process of discernment requires continuity with the past, careful listening in the present, and confidence that God will continue to meet us in the future. It also means that we need not fear culture as if its cacophonous noise could somehow silence the voice of God.

Culture as world: theology from *culture.* Whereas theology *of* culture tends to move from theology toward culture, my next preposition moves in the opposite direction. It seeks to discern the imaginative universe implicit in various cultural artifacts. When I am teaching my students to examine their favorite bits of pop culture, I begin with the basic categories of storytelling:

- What is the story (or stories) at the simplest level?
- What role does the medium (method of delivery) play in making the story work?
- Why does the larger culture resonate with this story?
- Why do I resonate with this story?

You will notice that none of these questions evaluate the stories of culture for their compatibility with the Christian worldview. That comes later. I should say that my students are quite ready to engage in worldview critique, at least at a basic level. They can tell me countless ways that their beloved shows, songs, and video games miss the mark (usually due to profanity, sex, and violence). Since I am a theology professor, that must be what I want to hear. But I find that their ability to engage in worldview critique does not often diminish their love for the artifacts they are criticizing, nor does it alter their ritual habits of watching, listening, or playing.

This is because our habits go deeper than our critical intellect. They are rooted in our cultural imagination. We consume culture in ways that fit our narrative identities, the stories we tell ourselves about ourselves. We are drawn to cultural artifacts that resonate with who we imagine ourselves to be and our sense of where we fit in the world. Cultural critique is necessary. But the first movement in engagement must be one of understanding: not just understanding why others resonate with this piece of culture, but why *I* resonate with it (or why I resist it).

Culture is not something "out there" that we can easily evaluate and selectively appropriate in accordance with untainted tenets of faith. What we call our worldview is already deeply enculturated, cast in terms of language, metaphors, and world-pictures with which we resonate. This is not a bad thing; it is a human thing. It is remarkable that God's Word can be translated into every cultural setting, becoming intelligible for us even as it brings a critique of our cultural idolatries. But since we are so deeply embedded in culture, it means that the work of discernment is a work that happens first in our own hearts, and our own communities, as we seek to understand the things that move us and matter most to us.

Theology and culture, after all, share many of the same concerns. They are the big questions that most humans ask:

- What kind of a place is this world?
- Which is the deeper reality: beauty or brutality?
- What is really worth living for?
- Who will help me make my way in the world?
- How do we live together amid deep differences?
- Where is this all going? Anywhere? What happens in the end?

These are questions that our cultural priests and poets are invested in exploring. Popular culture is already having this conversation, a conversation that is deeply theological, even if only implicitly. But if we follow these questions far enough, we will be confronted by more explicitly theological questions:

- Is there a God?
- What is God like?
- How does God matter?
- How would we get to know this God?
- What claims does this God make on my life?

To do theology *from* culture means to pay attention to the ways that cultural artifacts wrestle with these questions, offering challenges and connections for theology's more traditional sources. These challenges also require some sort of response. This leads to our third preposition.

Culture as web: theology for *culture.* It is easy for us to assume that the conversation between theology and culture mainly concerns our evaluation of someone else's work, someone else's worldview. But neither theology nor culture are affairs for detached analysis. Remember my earlier definition: theology is about what is most real and what really matters. Theology and culture win us to their vision of the world by aiming at our imagination (the "eyes of the heart"). Applied to cultural agency, this leads us to ask questions that set cultural artifacts in a larger context:

- Where do we see glimmers of beauty, goodness, and truth? How can we place this cultural artifact in the biblical story, manifesting created goodness, fallenness, or hope of redemption?
- Where do we see a cultural idolatry—a good thing that has been made into the ultimate thing?
- What challenge, critique, or completion might the gospel bring? How might the gospel offer fuller meaning?
- What will I make of this? How will this be woven into my life?

This last question is perhaps the most important one. Ultimately, our interpretation of culture is not just the judgments we make about it (theology of culture) but how we take it up (theology from culture) and how we steward it in our life together (theology for culture).

Another way to say this is, "Your interpretation is your life." I will return to this idea in the conclusion, but for now it is enough to say that we are all cultural interpreters. We are already engaged in countless acts of interpretation as we navigate the world. The best way to know my interpretation of a biblical text or cultural trend is to watch how I live with it, how I live it out in my daily life with others. To return to the opening example, after my youth group student threw his music into the river, life continued, and with it, countless daily decisions needed to be made. Should he listen to the radio while he gets ready for school? Should he purchase new, explicitly "Christian" music? When his friend shares a song with him, what should he do? When he writes music of his own, what should it sound like? These decisions are unavoidable, presenting themselves to us in concrete forms, the presence of significant others with whom we make our way, the ones that make us who we are: our family, community, and people.

And while everyday life requires us to take these significant others into account, theology's special burden is to remind us that God is the first significant other before whom, with whom, and for whom we live (Rom. 11:36). Living before God's face prepares us to live with integrity and skill in our cultural settings. In this sense, theology directs us to care for culture: serving others, planting seeds, offering our work to the Lord, anticipating that God will meet us in surprising ways. As Japanese American artist Makoto Fujimura reminds us, this is long and slow work, requiring generational faithfulness: "Theology must grow and be sown into the soils of culture, be fed by spring rains of love to be cultivated in multiple generations."[18] Theology is meant to orient us for our cultural task by providing us with a comprehensive vision, the story of the world in three movements: creation, fall, and redemption.[19] It aims to help us feel Christian meaning, see Christian truth, and practice Christian virtue. The goal is that we would weave webs of vitality, ways of life that are beautiful and nourishing, in which vulnerable members are knit into our communities of care. Becoming the sort of people who can do this means becoming more skillful in our lived interpretations. We must both train our intuitions and integrate a slower, more deliberate approach, distinguished by the theological virtues of faith, hope, and love (1 Cor. 13:13).

We begin with faith: faith that God has not abandoned the creation he loves, faith that God still speaks through Word and Spirit, that God still shows up in unexpected places, and that no matter what happens, the world belongs to God. We continue with hope, the conviction that God is turning the world right-side up and making all things new. This hope, grounded as it is on the life, death, and resurrection of Jesus Christ, gives us confidence that things can change and that what we do matters (1 Cor. 15:58). Finally, we proceed with love, directed toward the neighbors who bear the divine image, neighbors in whom we can discern sparks of glory even amid our shared depravity. To engage in theology *for* culture is to bring the resources of theology to bear on our cultural task: to take whatever inkling of good we can find at the outset and seek to nudge it in the direction of God's good future, with the hope that only the gospel can offer.

Culture as Literary Text: An Orienting Metaphor

My own orientation to the theological interpretation of culture came in the form of a class I took during my first semester of seminary: Cultural Hermeneutics. I didn't know what it meant, but I was intrigued by a class that included the word "culture" in its title. On the first day of class, it became clear that I was out of my depth. I had never even heard the term "cultural mandate," and I had never imagined that studying culture could be so sophisticated. And yet I was hooked. The class gave me categories, language, and methods to direct and discipline my ministry intuitions.

The professor, Kevin Vanhoozer, taught us to approach culture in the same way one might approach a literary text: "a world and work of meaning." Hermeneutics, he taught us, was the art of understanding; it required careful listening. This meant that rather than moving immediately to critique, we first had to understand culture on its own terms, to grasp the worlds of meaning contained in cultural texts and the way they work their way into our imagination. Cultural literacy opened the door to responsible cultural agency. For Christians to be faithful disciples, he told us, it was not enough for us to be wise interpreters of Scripture; we also needed to become wise interpreters of culture. The content of the class formed the basis of an important essay by Vanhoozer, which was published along with a collection of student essays (including one of my own) in a volume called *Everyday Theology*. In it, he frames the project's aim as transformative: "Everyday theology is nothing less than the attempt to understand everyday life: to see it as God sees it and, with God's help, to be an agent of redemptive change."[20]

To say that the class altered the course of my life is an understatement. Indeed, it is doubtful that I would have become a professor without it. Almost two decades later, I continue to find myself entranced by the conversation. And yet, I have also come to feel the limitations of the literary metaphor. The value of approaching culture as a text is that it leads us to look for meaning. But the drawback of this approach to "reading culture" is that it could produce an illusion of critical distance that we do not have—as William Dyrness puts it, "an isolated scholar sitting alone in her/his office grappling with a written text, or, in this case, an isolated cultural product."[21] In this picture, we wrestle with the text, deciding what it means, what ideas we can accept, and what ideas we should reject. But the reality is that culture is not just *communicative* but also *communicable*. It is caught before it is taught, and we investigate its meaning as those already in its grip.

I should say that Vanhoozer's account is nuanced, aware of the limitations of the metaphor, with resources for avoiding the "isolationist" approach that Dyrness fears.[22] All metaphors have limitations, and it is for this reason that I have sought not to *replace* the literary metaphor but to *emplace* it among other metaphors and methods of cultural engagement. In this understanding, cultural interpretation requires a kaleidoscope, and in the chapters that follow, I explore cultural life through five lenses:

1. The Meaning Dimension: *Culture as Immune System*
2. The Power Dimension: *Culture as Power Play*
3. The Ethical Dimension: *Culture as Moral Boundary*
4. The Religious Dimension: *Culture as Sacred Experience*
5. The Aesthetic Dimension: *Culture as Poetic Project*

Each of these approaches has something significant to offer, and none of them can be reduced to the others. Culture is how we make meaning in the world, but culture is not just a matter of meaning; it is also about power. On the other hand, culture is not reducible to power. There is also more to culture making than coping or moralizing. The burden of this book is to show how each discipline needs the others, and how they all need theology. In each chapter, theology is brought to bear as an integrative discipline, a host who opens space for others, while also keeping any one voice from dominating the conversation. To that end, I will highlight a distinctive practice corresponding to each cultural dimension: hospitality, iconoclasm, servanthood, discernment, and making.

This book offers a non-anxious approach to cultural engagement, one that is attentive to the hunger for meaning, beauty, and justice and is governed by gospel virtues of faith, love, and hope. It invites readers to join ongoing conversations between theology and culture by listening, learning, and speaking with a distinctively Christian voice. It offers a multilayered approach, attending not just to what culture says but also to what it does and what we do with it: how it forms us as political actors, how it moves us aesthetically, how it shapes the rhythms of our lives, and how it connects us with the God and neighbor we have been called to love. For, to borrow from the apostle, the end of our cultural interpretation is not just understanding but "love, which comes from a pure heart and a good conscience and a sincere faith" (1 Tim. 1:5).

QUESTIONS FOR REFLECTION AND DISCUSSION

1. How do you locate yourself culturally? What are the communities of which you consider yourself a member? What are the different layers of cultural identity that have formed who you are?

2. This chapter opened with stories about engaging the culture of youth group students, including one student who threw all his secular CDs in the river. Do you have any memorable stories about the interaction of theology and culture in your own life?

3. This chapter distinguishes three prepositions for describing the conversation between theology and culture: "of," "from," and "for." What has been your basic preposition or posture in relating theology and culture? What other prepositions could be added (e.g., "against," "with"), and what posture results from each preposition?

4. What are the strengths and weaknesses of thinking about cultural artifacts as a "text"? Are there other metaphors for culture that would be worth exploring?

THE MEANING DIMENSION

Culture as Immune System

As I write this sentence, the world reels from the novel coronavirus (SARS-CoV-2) and its variants, which cause the disease popularly known as COVID-19. It is impossible to quantify all the ways that COVID has changed our world. It is also impossible to avoid it at the beginning of this book about culture. Discussions of culture tend to focus on human agency and our arts of making: the way we make places, artifacts, and institutions as part of the larger project of making meaning. I will follow this trajectory. But the coronavirus is a reminder that culture making always takes place within concrete, creaturely limitations.

We are beings with bodies, embedded in communities, living in a particular time and place. These particularities both enable what we make and limit what we can do. Chief among our limits are certain biological realities. We must eat, we need to rest, and we are susceptible to illness. Even as we marshal our best efforts to cope with, contain, and cure disease, its power often exceeds our collective resources. Viruses humble us. They remind us that despite our best attempts to manage our fragility, there are some things that remain beyond our capacity to control. Death is the finite horizon against which all culture making is set. Whatever meaning we make, whatever innovations we achieve, we do so in the knowledge that our bodies will eventually break down and our experience of the world—with all its meaning—will end. Theology speaks of a hope beyond that end, and of a human vocation before that end. But the end itself is not in doubt.

How do we make our way in this brutal, beautiful world? And how do we account for its beauty and brutality? In this chapter I will reflect on the meaning dimension of culture using a biological analogy: culture as virus and immune system. This analogy seeks to capture both the virality and vitality of culture. Bits of culture may spread like viruses, but when many bits of culture come together as a complex whole,[1] culture works more like an immune system, a dynamic system of discernment. I will argue that our resonance with particular cultural strains (and our resistance to others) has to do with the experience of meaning, which offers us security and stability in an uncertain world. I will then situate the discussion within three theological frames: (1) ecosystem and exile, (2) purity and pollution, and (3) Spirit and community. My goal in this chapter will be to explore the way that culture works both like a virus and like an immune system, and how the "good infection" of the gospel seeks to heal the human community.

Going Viral: The Virality and Vitality of Culture

Let us begin with the virality of culture. Although we have good reason for thinking of viruses as vicious, this is not always true; viruses can regulate bacterial populations or carry genes that are beneficial to their hosts.[2] In any case, the point of speaking about culture's virality is not that culture is a harmful *contagion*, but that culture is *contagious*, caught before it is taught.[3] Our everyday use of this metaphor (e.g., "the post went viral") captures an intuition about how culture reproduces and spreads. Indeed, there is a tradition within sociobiology that describes human culture using biotic categories. For these thinkers, virality is more than a metaphor; it is an attempt to ground culture in the basic struggle of organisms to survive in complex environments.[4] Using these categories, cognitive scientist Merlin Donald describes culture as something that "invades us and sets our agendas."[5] Although this perspective may minimize human agency—what we do with culture—the potency of thinking about culture as a virus is precisely the way that it refuses to grant us critical distance. Just as those who study a virus are susceptible to infection, so too those who study culture are already exposed, inhabiting environments rich with viral strains.

Here a brief foray into virology may be instructive. Viruses are microscopic pieces of genetic information that worm their way into living cells, like lines of rogue computer code. The coronavirus belongs to a group of viruses identifiable by the crown-like spikes on their surface. Each spike is a key of sorts, in search of a lock. When it finds an opening, it can gain entry to the cell, and once inside it instructs the cell to reproduce the viral code. As the cell replicates the virus, there are sometimes transcription errors in the code, and this produces new strains. These variants make some viruses extremely difficult to eradicate, often with devastating effects for their hosts.

We are vulnerable to viruses, but we are not without protections. Humans have developed complex immune systems to discern and defend their bodies against invaders. The immune system seeks to deny viral entry and to stop viral spread if entry is gained. It accomplishes this second mission by fighting the virus with white blood cells and antibodies that will remember the virus and keep it from wreaking havoc a second time. Some viruses, like the coronavirus, work by turning the immune system against itself, leading to a breakdown of the body's vital functions.

It is not difficult to see why sociobiologists have used this basic paradigm of virality to describe the way that culture multiplies and mutates. Culture, too, is composed of countless bits of "code," embedded in ideas and artifacts, stories and customs, images and institutions. These cultural traces seek willing hosts who will entertain them, take them up, and transcribe them in new ways. It is not for nothing that "going viral" is the longing of every aspiring YouTube star, influencer, or brand ambassador. Virality means that you have found a key that unlocks, at least for a moment, the attention of millions.

Long before he became one of the "four horsemen" of the new atheism, British biologist Richard Dawkins coined the word "meme": an idea or trend that spreads throughout a culture like a virus.[6] Though the field of "memetics" has struggled to win recognition from empirically minded scientists, the internet has taken the meme concept in dizzying directions, multiplying images, GIFs, and other strains of culture that spread like a wildfire. Memes have become a world of meaning unto themselves. Not long ago I had a student who created a final project in which he used internet memes to retell the story of the Bible. I appreciated the creativity, but the way the rest of the class laughed throughout the presentation made me feel like I was missing something, as if memes were a language I did not speak, a novel way of describing the world in which I had been insufficiently immersed.

But not everything goes viral; we are not merely at the mercy of memes. And here we can turn to the other side of the metaphor: culture as an immune system. To use Kevin Vanhoozer's categories from the introduction, if the virus is an image of culture as a *work* of meaning—communicative and communicable—the immune system is an image of culture as a *world* of meaning, one that forms a community. In the latter case, culture provides us with a dynamic system of discernment, one that allows us to move through an ocean of information and yet maintain a unified identity. We are more likely to entertain bits of culture that fit the narrative of who we've been (our cultural history), who we believe ourselves to be (our cultural identity), and who we want to become (our cultural aspiration).

When I lived in Southern California, one of my favorite places to eat was Grand Central Market in downtown Los Angeles. The market is known for the diversity of its food options, representing many of the cultures that make up LA's metropolitan center. To walk through the market is to experience a feast for the senses: sights, sounds, smells, and tastes. Some of the scents are unfamiliar; others are enticing. Some remind me of the way our kitchen smelled while I was growing up; others remind me of places I've visited; still others remind me of my friends. Smelling is free, but eventually I must choose a place to have a meal. I may choose something based on its novelty or based on its familiarity. But my identity—who I am, where I was raised, where I've been, who I've befriended, how I see myself—privileges certain smells over others, making the possibility of stopping at certain places more likely. This is true for us whether we prefer what is familiar or whether we are more adventurous. I once explored the streets of Hong Kong with a friend. I was in search of noodles; he was in search of McDonald's. I was incredulous, but I will never forget his response: "It makes me feel at home."

Why do some things cling to us while others do not? I want to argue that the strength of the bond we feel to particular cultural strains has to do with the experience of meaning. Like the crowns of a virus, pieces of culture hook into our hearts. Some of culture's viral variants mesh with our cultural immune system. They name, organize, or validate our experience, and when they do, they offer us—even momentarily—a more stable space where we can stand.

Meaning is an elusive concept to define—what does meaning *mean*? I am using it here to refer to the experience of connection, resonance, and recognition that we feel as we move through the world. Sometimes this experience is pleasant and predictable, such as when I find my "place" in a familiar chair. Other times the experience is pleasant but surprising, such as when I recognize the face of a friend in a crowded airport. Other times the experience of meaning is unpleasant, such as when I see flashing lights in the rearview mirror. And sometimes it is difficult for us to explain why we feel so intensely, such as when a song summons unexpected tears. In any case, we let cultural stories take up residence in our bones because it seems to us that these stories capture something important about the world and our place within it.

Culture clings to us because it *means* something to us. And we are fundamentally creatures who need meaning to survive. We constantly seek connections between our outer and inner worlds, and to find this resonance, we develop a poetic ability to unlock the symbolic, meaning-rich quality of the world. We shape light and sound into images, songs, and stories; we shape the raw materials of creation into physical objects; we shape our social environments into communities and movements. Thus, the world of human culture is born: an ecosystem of signification. As anthropologist Clifford Geertz memorably put it, we are suspended in webs of significance that we ourselves have spun. This means (at least for Geertz) that cultural analysis is not "an experimental science in search of law but an interpretive one in search of meaning."[7]

This image of being suspended among many threads of significance is a powerful one. Imagine returning to your hometown after a decade living in another place. Everywhere you go, you feel the threads of meaning connecting you to that place. Perhaps the threads are fraying, no longer as taut as they once were, but the tethers are still there. Familiar faces and places secure your sense of fit, how at home you feel in this corner of the world. Now imagine traveling to another country and being dropped in a random neighborhood. The place is unfamiliar, and the customs are strange; you do not even speak the language. Here the tethers are few, and your sense of fit is fragile. There is still a human connection to be made and meaning to be shared, perhaps through facial expressions and hand gestures. But the web of meaning is tenuous, leaving you with the feeling that you are floating in space.

We gravitate toward the bits of culture that strengthen our sense of fit, those that enable us to have some degree of stability in the world. Naturally, there will be some cultural strains to which we will develop an allergic reaction, ideas and impressions for which we have built up a powerful resistance because they destabilize our sense that we are safe. Perhaps these pieces of culture come from the rival political party, or from those outside our group. Our cultural discernment apparatus kicks into gear, identifying these strains as a threat, and denying them residence in our imagination. But there are other cultural traces whose keys seem to fit our locks. We feel an immediate sense of resonance, recognition, and connection. And so that viral bit of cultural code enters the cell, becoming a part of our cultural immune system.

We can see the power of an immune system analysis when we consider the way that people process information about contested issues. The modern ideal is that we will draw conclusions based on data, develop positions based on facts, and group ourselves with others who share our apprehension of reality. But social-scientific research indicates that the actual process is almost exactly the reverse. We first identify with a team (it usually chooses us), assume the positions of our team, and then interpret the world in a way that fits the team's predilections.[8] In other words, belonging comes before believing.

Social psychologist Jonathan Haidt argues that human reason behaves less like an impartial judge and more like a defense attorney; when confronted with new information, it seeks to resolve the danger by reinterpreting the data. He cites a study—conducted just prior to an American presidential election—that monitored the brain activity of self-identified "highly partisan" Democrats and Republicans as they were presented with damaging information about their candidate. For subjects on both sides, the conscious-reasoning part of the brain *failed* to activate, while the emotional centers went into overdrive, as if perceiving an attack.

The point is that when we feel threatened, we are nearly unteachable; rather than challenging our biases, we become increasingly rigid. This means, Haidt writes, that we develop the ability to believe almost anything that supports our team.[9] The flourishing of conspiracy theories, which have gone mainstream in American culture, bears this out. When it comes to cultural discernment, we can become immunocompromised too, unable to distinguish between reputable and disreputable sources, between legitimate and fake news, or between ordinary bias and outright propaganda.

Our cultural gullibility is unsurprising if what we are after is not primarily truth but stable *meaning*, centered in the security of our group and personal identities. This stability is caught up in the health of our cultural immune system. Problems occur, of course, when one immune system goes to war with another—when I see the inhabitants of another bubble endangering my own. We often speak of the echo chambers we tend to curate, spaces where everyone affirms and agrees with our basic vision of the world. But casting culture as an immune system captures the way we feel compromised, threatened, and fragile, not so much by the viral bits of culture we instinctively reject, but by the rival immune systems that represent wholly different ways of being in the world. What do we do when it dawns on us that there are others who are allergic to the very things that we hold most dear?

I teach at a Christian university located in a rural community in the midwestern United States. Our student body is more diverse than you might imagine, yet many of my students testify to the experience of living in what they call a "Christian bubble." What they mean by this is that they are aware that their life experiences have been uniquely local, insulated from the larger world. Sometimes students lament what they perceive as a narrowness of vision within the bubble. Other times they express gratitude for the sense that they have solid ground on which to stand. But the awareness of a "bubble" includes the recognition that there are other ways of being in the world that are not only possible but often desirable. In any case, contact with other webs of meaning can make our own web feel much more fragile, endangered, and exposed.

In his three-part magnum opus, *Spheres*, German philosopher Peter Sloterdijk tells a story of humans in search of "immune system bubbles"— which allow us to feel stable and safe in an inhospitable world. He sees the story of modernity as the effort to create new, industrial-grade immune systems to replace the (theologically inspired) spheres of meaning that we have lost. Having lost the insulating safety that theology once provided, we now find ourselves exposed to the elements, without a shell. He writes, "Modernity is characterized by the technical production of its immunities and the increasing removal of its safety structures from the traditional theological and cosmological narratives. Industrial-scale civilization, the welfare state, the world market and the media sphere: all these large-scale projects aim, in a shelless time, for an imitation of the now impossible, imaginary spheric security. Now networks and insurance policies are meant to replace the celestial domes; telecommunications has to re-enact the all-encompassing. The body of humanity seeks to create a new immune constitution in electronic media skin."[10] In other words, what makes us feel secure? No longer is it religious stories of our place in a meaning-filled cosmos, but instead it is "industrial-scale civilization." Civilization here is a globalizing force, but paradoxically, our overextended connectedness—which sensitizes us to innumerable threats at home and abroad—makes us feel less secure. Mimicking another German philosopher, Karl Marx (whom we will revisit in chap. 2), Sloterdijk retells the story of civilization not as a narrative of class struggle but as "the history of immune system bubbles." Either the bubbles collapse, causing crisis, or the bubbles coalesce into a more poetic "foam": this is his image for the possibility of life amid plurality.

We do not need to agree with Sloterdijk's grand story to appreciate the explanatory force of his metaphor.[11] And we can learn at least two things from him. First, we cannot answer the question "Who are we?" without the question "Where are we?" and its corollary questions, "Where do we fit?" and "Where are we secure?" Second, our sense of certainty in answering these questions is compromised, constantly being called into question through encounters with cultural others. The collision of rival worlds of meaning need not be violent, but violence is always a possibility. In a pluralistic world, it is incumbent on all to mine their tradition in search of resources that will push us toward healthy pluralism and peace.

Christians believe that peace is possible for one reason: God has not abandoned creation to corruption. As Paul preached to the Lycaonians who mistook him for Hermes, the real God has never been "without witness," providing "rain from heaven, and fruitful seasons, filling our hearts with food and gladness" (Acts 14:17 KJV). For despite the temporary shelter our technological bubbles provide, when it comes to meaning they are a poor substitute for the metaphysical thickness of theology. Modern culture's detachment from the tapestry of transcendence has led to a sense of unease. Hyperaware of the webs we have woven—and the webs others have woven for us—we despair at whether our connection to others or to the world is really meaningful after all.

But the revelation of God in Jesus compels us to claim that we are also caught up in threads of meaning not made by human hands (Heb. 9:11). There are creational structures in which we live, a creaturely vocation that we cannot help but fulfill, and a Creator who pursues us with redeeming love. Grounding human culture in these divine gifts does not rob culture of its human element. Rather it roots our cultural life in a better soil, securing us to something more solid than ourselves, offering a stability that death itself cannot shake. In the next section we will pull on three theological threads that plumb the search for an immune system that will provide security in the face of our vulnerability to viruses, both terrestrial and infernal.

Theological Thread 1: Ecosystem and Exile

Scripture opens with the story of God making a place where humanity can live in God's presence. The result is a world of creaturely meaning, an ecosystem of interdependence. Light and darkness, separated on day one, host the waters above and below, separated on day two. The waters host the dry land, created on day three. The skies, waters, and land act as hosts for living things. As James Skillen shows, each of God's creatures "has a unique, irreducible place of honor, and tied to that honor is the service of hospitality toward other creatures."[12] Human beings, created in God's image and called to cultivate creation, fulfill their vocation through hospitality: first, through hosting the Creator who speaks, and second, by showing honor to all God's creatures (and here light and land are equally God's creatures) in faithful stewardship of creation. To live within this ecosystem of interdependent creatures—all of whom are dependent on the Creator—is to share in God's Sabbath rest. Together the human family is meant to function like a good infection, multiplying and maximizing the joy throughout creation.

Immediately following this exalted vision (Gen. 1) is a complementary narrative from a more intimate gaze (Gen. 2). God forms an earthling (*'adam*) from the dust of the earth (*'adamah*) and then kisses this clay creation with animating breath. The inspired human is then placed within a fruited plain and called to "guard and keep" the garden that God has planted (Gen. 2:15). Using Sloterdijk's language, we can think of Eden as an immune system bubble, an ecosystem where what is good flourishes and what is evil is resisted, as defined by the only One with the prerogative to say which is which. The divine prerogative to make such pronouncements is represented in the tree of the knowledge of good and evil.

But in Genesis 3 a foreign element is introduced, through a serpent whose viral voice tells the humans that they should decide what is good and evil for themselves. Later in Scripture the serpent will be identified as a fallen evil power (Rev. 12:9), but the point in Genesis is that the voice comes from the cunning of creaturely wisdom rather than from the Creator (Gen. 3:1), while also reversing the creation order in which humanity exercises dominion. Upon Adam and Eve's act of creaturely rebellion, the bubble of blessing is pierced. Humanity is exiled from the garden, compelled to make their way in a creation that is no longer altogether hospitable. Culture making will now take place amid thorns and thistles and will be fraught with anxiety: "By the sweat of your face you shall eat bread" (Gen. 3:19 ESV). Old Testament scholar Sandra Richter writes that rather than reading "sweat" as an idiom for hard work, it is instead a statement of "perspiration-inducing fear": "What we find in Genesis 3 is that because of the rebellion of the earth and the expulsion of Adam and Eve from God's presence, humanity will now live their lives in an adversarial world with a constant, gnawing undercurrent of dread that there will not be enough, that their labor will not meet the need. . . . This is the curse of *'Adam*—limited resources, an insecure future and a world that no longer responds to my command."[13] The expulsion from the ecosystem of Eden means increased instability. And anxiety is warranted, because separation from the tree of life will entail a return to the dust: "For you are dust, and to dust you shall return" (Gen. 3:19 ESV). The bubble of every human life is subject to the puncture of death, as God withdraws his animating breath.

The remainder of the biblical story can be understood after this pattern of ecosystem and exile, as humanity seeks a new ecosystem and struggles with the wound of exile. Adam and Eve remain in the region of Eden, though not in the garden. But after killing his brother, Cain sets out for the wild places of the world, "east of Eden," "away from the presence of the LORD" (Gen. 4:16 ESV). Genesis describes him as a restless wanderer (*na*) who wanders (*vanad*) in the land of wandering (*Nod*). He is the first to build a city—a technological ecosystem—and his descendants are distinguished by their skill in culture making. Jabal is adept at animal husbandry, Jubal at music, and Tubal-Cain at forging all sorts of tools (Gen. 4:20–22). Culture making (the work of meaning) continues in a fallen condition. How could it not? But insofar as it is done "away from the presence of the LORD," it will now be fraught with anxiety, misdirected, out of sync with a world that no longer yields its strength. The abiding cultural temptation—epitomized in the Tower of Babel (Gen. 11)—will be to place our trust in the work of our hands rather than to find security in the promise of God.

At this point, filmmaker Darren Aronofsky's cinematic retelling of the flood story in the film *Noah* places a memorable speech in the mouth of Tubal-Cain: "The Creator does not care what happens in this world. Nobody has heard from Him since He marked Cain. We are alone. Orphaned children, cursed to struggle by the sweat of our brow to survive. Damned if I don't do everything it takes to do just that. Damned if I don't take what I want."[14] A dramatic flourish not found in the biblical text, it nevertheless captures exiled humanity's desperation and depravity. Created to unfold creation's beauty, Cain's descendants instead fill the earth with violence. Rather than spreading love and justice, humanity functions more like a malignant infection. In the flood, God steps in to stop the spread of evil, to quarantine the contagion and wipe it out. The language of Genesis 6:7, "I will blot out man whom I have created" (ESV), is clearly an image of purification that is followed by the cleansing flood that reverts the earth from ordered cosmos to watery chaos.

This pattern of ecosystem and exile continues to echo through the rest of the biblical story. The cultural mandate has not been revoked: humanity and human culture multiply and spread. We are still responsible to make our way in the world, and we still seek to create spaces where we can survive and flourish. We make clothes to cover our nakedness and build cities to protect ourselves from danger. But now we do so in competition with other creatures, organized into immune systems at war with other immune systems. Instead of honor and hospitality, we are prone toward rivalry and hostility, counting some more worthy of life than others. Meaning making continues but is twisted by sin. As a result, cultural customs may be coherent to us and yet be ill-fitting with God's intended vision, like an instrument that is in tune with itself but dissonant with a true tone. Just so, for humanity has turned—like Cain—away from the face of the Lord.

But God has not turned away from humanity. For there is no place humans can hide from God's face (Ps. 139:7: "Where shall I go from your Spirit? Or where shall I flee from your presence?" [ESV]; see also Ps. 10:11; Isa. 47:10; Jer. 23:24). Despite the line that Aronofsky writes for Tubal-Cain, God does not even abandon Cain's line. The mark on Cain is intended to preserve his life. And though his descendants seem outside God's covenantal purposes, God graciously allows them to live, multiply, and develop culture, excelling in the making of music and tools. This suggests that after the exile from Eden, cultural projects are complex, ambiguous phenomena. They are easily tilted toward evil, becoming contagions unto themselves. They are even capable of arriving at a point of summative judgment (a judgment only God can make). But it would be wrong to say that humanity's making always misses the mark.

God's work outside the walls of the covenantal community is mysterious to us, and we should be careful about too quickly identifying God's fingerprints or footsteps. But we can say categorically, with Dutch theologian Herman Bavinck, "There exists a rich revelation of God even among the heathen—not only in nature but also in their heart and conscience, in their life and history, among their statesmen and artists, their philosophers and reformers. There exists no reason at all to denigrate or diminish this divine revelation. . . . All that is good and true has its origin in grace, including the good we see in fallen man. The light still does shine in darkness. The spirit of God makes its home and works in all the creation."[15] The world still belongs to God, and every human being bears God's image. Thus, we should not be surprised to find beauty, goodness, and truth everywhere. For out of incredible generosity and grace, God sends humanity "good dreams," offering innumerable clues in creation, conscience, and culture, even if those clues are suppressed and not followed back to the source of life.[16]

We are also reminded, in the early chapters of Genesis, that the desperation of Cain is not the only option: "At that time people began to call upon the name of the LORD" (4:26). The way of Cain and the tower builders of Babylon is not the only way to live in an unfriendly, inhospitable world. There is another way: to call on the name of the Lord, resting in his promises and following his direction as we make our way in an uncertain and unsafe world.

Theological Thread 2: Purity and Pollution

This brings us to my second theological thread, which I will draw out from a less-traveled part of the story: the cultic regulations of Leviticus. The Levitical code is the part of the Bible that makes readers feel its cultural strangeness, often leaving it unexamined and unread. And yet, when we place Leviticus within this pattern of ecosystem and exile, a fascinating picture emerges. Within the covenant people of God—those who call on the name of the Lord—cultural skill is leveraged to make a new place for God's presence. Bezalel is filled with God's Spirit/breath "to make artistic designs for work in gold, silver and bronze, to cut and set stones, to work in wood, and to engage in all kinds of crafts" (Exod. 31:4–5) for the sake of the tabernacle. The cultic regulations in the book of Leviticus represent elaborate measures to preserve the purity of tabernacle, whereby God dwells with his people.

This is a critical point: not every cultural product remains purely a work of human hands. Some cultural products are taken up into the divine economy of redemption. Humans make clothing for themselves, but there are also garments made, in some sense, by God (Gen. 3:7, 21). Likewise, humans make immune system bubbles for themselves, but some spaces are made by God—through human hands—so that humanity can live in God's presence. This does not make those cultural works less human; it represents God sanctifying human creative work for holy purposes. This is a divine intervention, one that comes from the outside (it is transcendent in source) and yet makes itself intelligible through human culture.

The supreme example of this in the Old Testament is the tabernacle, and later the temple. In the construction of the tabernacle, we have a return to the Edenic ecosystem. From the garden imagery in the furnishings to the cherubim that guard the mercy seat, entry into the Holy of Holies on the Day of Atonement reverses the movement away from God's presence.[17] This leads Old Testament scholar L. Michael Morales to cast the core drama of Leviticus in this way: "A sacred bubble has been set within a sea of uncleanness; how now may any Israelite, when even his lungs are polluted, enter this sphere? And how may the sphere be kept clean continually?"[18]

At the risk of oversimplification, the question of purity and pollution situates the entire Levitical law code. The normal condition of fallen humanity is uncleanness, and thus purification is necessary for God's presence to continue to dwell among his people. There are levels to this: moral failures that require forgiveness, while ritual impurities require cleansing. Since humans are subject to and saturated by death, purification is needed to enter the place of life. A skin disease like leprosy or the loss of life's fluids through menstruation or intercourse created ritual impurity. Impurity is cleansed in some cases by water, and in other cases by blood, for "life . . . is in the blood" (Lev. 17:11). The heart of Leviticus is the story of how the tabernacle absorbs the impurity and expels it from the community on the Day of Atonement.

When it comes to the shape of Israel's immune system bubble—its common life, centered on the tabernacle—purity and pollution are conceived in the most tangible of terms. To put it plainly, it is less about religious feelings and more about bodily fluids. As Stanley Hauerwas has remarked, "Any religion that does not tell you what to do with your genitals and pots and pans cannot be interesting."[19] The Levitical laws do not descend from heaven; their intricate scaffolding emerges from Israel's intuitions about practicing divine presence amid the everyday realities of life and death. And yet, these laws bear the stamp of divine authority, taken up in the divine economy and accepted as fitting action for dwelling safely with God.

Christians believe that the Levitical laws are no longer meant to be observed in their scrupulous detail. Though an integral part of the story, they are not the part of the story we are in; we cannot read them apart from the sending of Jesus and the Spirit. The point of this discussion is to highlight the vital connection between *cult* (things associated with worship) and *culture* (things associated with ordinary human work). For the biblical authors, security and stability can only be found when a community's everyday life is properly oriented around God. In the Old Testament, the continuing threat is that if Israel becomes polluted by idolatry and injustice, the land itself "will vomit you out" (Lev. 18:28). The desire for a "spacious place" (Ps. 18:19) where we can "dwell securely" (Ezek. 28:26 ESV) is a basic human longing. Aware of the fact that we are subject to death and disease, all communities pursue purity of various sorts, developing intuitions and judgments on what (and who) is clean. Indeed, Haidt identifies the concern for purity (what he calls "Sanctity/degradation") as one of six foundational moral intuitions found in all human cultures. He writes, "The Sanctity/degradation foundation evolved initially in response to the adaptive challenge of the omnivore's dilemma [the idea that omnivores can explore new food sources while also remaining wary of them], and then to the broader challenge of living in a world of pathogens and parasites. It includes the behavioral immune system, which can make us wary of a diverse array of symbolic objects and threats. It makes it possible for people to invest objects with irrational and extreme values—both positive and negative—which are important for binding groups together."[20] It is not just religions, Haidt points out, that invest ordinary things with "clean-unclean" distinctions. Objects like flags, places like the US Capitol building, and principles like freedom can all be "sanctified" or "desecrated." When desecration occurs, it is a violation that almost always leads to separation, expulsion, or cancellation, for the sake of the community's well-being.

If a scrupulous concern for purity seemed strange to us prior to the COVID-19 pandemic, perhaps now it is less so. Herein lies another paradox: some communities found the shift to widespread mask-wearing to be intuitive, representative of public health; others found it to be invasive, representative of government overreach. We can make sense of these disparate responses through our analogy of the immune system. We all inhabit cultural and ideological immune systems that are resistant to certain strains of thought and action. And these cultural immune systems can at times place our bodily immune systems in greater jeopardy.

Despite divergent cultural intuitions, there is always a sense of the clean and the common. This was reinforced to me a few years ago when I joined a CrossFit "box" (what CrossFitters call their social fitness centers). I found the culture of CrossFit to be incredibly fascinating. Fitness has always been a popular replacement for religion, but CrossFit has developed an "ecclesiology," an intentional community culture. When I joined the box, I noticed a sign that read, "Invite Your Friends to Experience Our Community." At my first class the other members noticed me and welcomed me; I thought to myself, "So this is how a new visitor feels when they come to church."

As I spent time in the church of CrossFit, however, I encountered something that made it more difficult to participate: food laws! CrossFitters eat according to a mantra: "meat and vegetables, nuts and seeds, some fruit, little starch, and no sugar." Many of the members observed special diets; in fact, they called it "eating clean," as in, "You eat pretty clean, don't you, Justin?" But clean eating can be inconvenient, even costly. Dietary restrictions separate you from others; it can be tough to go out to eat or drink with friends. The result was that my fellow CrossFitters tended to spend most of their time with other CrossFitters, who tended to share a similar diet, dress in similar attire, and place similar value on exercise.

This is the way cultural immune systems work. We naturally gravitate not just to ideas and impressions but also toward people who eat the same food, follow similar rhythms, and share similar sensibilities. There is something human and healthy about this: communities require something in common. But cultural difference also has a way of separating us from others who are not like us. Thick communities can become insular, difficult for outsiders to access. All of us can relate to the satisfaction of feeling like we *fit in* a community, as well as to the loneliness of feeling that we have been *left out*. Even if we never feel completely at home, one of the greatest joys in the world is to feel like "these are my people," to feel that we belong. But in a fallen world, this desire to belong can foster the dangerous intuition that *my* people are pure, and the ones outside my group are pollutants. This becomes apparent during times of crisis, especially pandemics, when it is always "foreigners" who are to blame. Violence nearly always follows, as the perceived pathogens are expelled from the cultural immune system.

Theological Thread 3: Spirit and Community

This brings us to the third theological thread. After the resurrection of Jesus, it is on the day of Pentecost (originally set aside to commemorate the gift of the law) that the Spirit is given to the church. Luke goes to great lengths to represent the diverse people groups who are present: "Parthians, Medes and Elamites; residents of Mesopotamia, Judea and Cappadocia, Pontus and Asia, Phrygia and Pamphylia, Egypt and the parts of Libya near Cyrene; visitors from Rome (both Jews and converts to Judaism); Cretans and Arabs" (Acts 2:9–11). As the Spirit empowers the believers to speak, each immigrant and pilgrim hears about the mighty works of God in their own language. This is the first sign of the rapidly expanding borders of God's family beyond the familiar. Since the time of the early church fathers, commentators have seen Pentecost as the dramatic reversal of the Tower of Babel. At Babel, humanity tried to build a tower to heaven; on Pentecost, heaven comes down. At Babel, human languages were confused; on Pentecost, the language barrier is supernaturally overcome. At Babel, the nations were scattered; on Pentecost, representatives from every nation are drawn together to hear the good news in their native tongue or, as Wycliffe Bible translators often put it, their "heart language."

The significance of the day of Pentecost for theology and culture cannot be overstated. The Spirit does not homogenize all languages into a universal tongue. Rather, each person hears his or her own native language. Diversity is affirmed and embraced; the cultural histories of these proselytes are taken up and grafted into the story of Jesus and the church.[21] From the very beginning, Christian mission has affirmed the dignity of every human culture, translating God's Word into every language, insisting that the Spirit has something to say to and through these people too.

It will take time for the church in Acts to come to terms with this paradigm-shattering miracle. It takes further revelation to resituate the code of what is clean and what is unclean: Peter's vision of a great sheet of animals descending from heaven. In the vision, he is instructed to join a meal: "Get up, Peter. Kill and eat" (Acts 10:13). The problem, of course, is that according to Levitical law, some of the animals were ceremonially unclean, representative of the dietary laws that created a distinction between Israel and surrounding peoples. Rabbinical deliberation added further restrictions, extending the category of cleanliness to clothing, furniture, and household. All of this led to a sharp division between Jews and gentiles. Table fellowship between them was out of the question: to get a sense of the visceral disgust, we might imagine sitting down next to someone who is eating a rat.

But Peter's vision calls his categories into question. When Peter protests, citing his scruples, he is told, "What God has made clean, do not call common" (Acts 10:15 ESV). Peter meets Cornelius and enters his house, and the meaning of the vision is plain. God is not necessarily asking Jewish Christians to break the kosher laws. God is asking them to break the association between clean and common food and clean and common people. The good news about Jesus is for everyone, without partiality to ethnicity, gender, or any other categories that humanity uses to separate and exclude.

If the pattern from Leviticus is that purification is required for God's presence to dwell among humanity, then perhaps we can say that the priestly work of Jesus makes two things possible. First, it makes possible the indwelling presence of the Spirit within and among the Christian community. But it also makes possible the translatability of the gospel into every human language, into a cultural idiom and logic that makes sense.

Here we can say that in addition to the infectious strains of meaning provided by culture and the church, there is an additional infusion of meaning: divine action through Jesus and the Spirit. C. S. Lewis describes the work of Christ in this way, working like a "good infection": "He came to this world and became a man in order to spread to other men the kind of life that He has. . . . If we get close to him, we shall catch it from Him."[22] In the incarnation, Jesus takes on our humanity. Dying, he destroys our death; rising, he restores our life. Through his ascension he brings our humanity into the very presence of God. Finally, through the gift of the Spirit, he prepares every culture to be a fitting "host" for the good infection of the gospel, seasoned by the "salt-like" proclamation of the church (Matt. 5:13; Col. 4:6).[23]

Conclusion: Fulfillment, Not Replacement

I conclude this discussion with two foundational axioms that will guide the rest of the conversation. First, every human culture is capable of "hosting" the gospel. Second, the gospel calls every human culture to repentance and the obedience of faith (Acts 17:30; Rom. 1:5). It confronts every culture with the revelation of God in Jesus Christ, a revelation that comes from the outside with a message we could not have told ourselves, even as it makes itself intelligible on the inside in the most intimate of terms. There will be cultural immune systems and idolatries that will make for a more hostile reception. Others will seek quickly to syncretize the gospel, thus rendering themselves more resistant to the gospel's leavening power. But no culture is so fallen that all its stories, systems, and significances need to be replaced without remainder. In fact, the heart of the approach pursued in this book can be summed up in the following phrase: fulfillment, not replacement. To be sure, the malignancy of sin must be removed. Cultural idolatries must be confronted. But everything that is truly human will be healed—along with all of creation—finding its fullness in the kingdom of God.[24]

My image for the relationship of theology and culture is a common one from the Gospels: Jesus in table fellowship. Indeed, it seems that no one was turned away when Jesus was at the table. No matter who you were, he would eat with you. This created a beautiful paradox, with Jesus bringing together two elements that were absolutely unique. On the one hand, his call to discipleship was of the highest order: die to yourself, take up your cross, follow me. On the other hand, Jesus attracted the most ordinary and imperfect people imaginable. Rather than being put off by Jesus's high standards, sinners and outsiders seemed to be particularly drawn to him. The result was a thick community that wrestled with the cost of discipleship while also remaining hospitable to outsiders.

I once heard New Testament scholar Scot McKnight say that what set Jesus apart from the Pharisees was their distinctive understandings of holiness. The Pharisees believed that holiness was something fragile to be protected; Jesus believed that holiness was something powerful to be unleashed. The Pharisees said, if you are clean, you can be with us; Jesus said, be with me, and you will become clean. Similarly, the approach pursued in this book assumes that what theology has to offer— the gospel—is not something fragile to be protected, but something powerful to be unleashed. This does not exempt us from the essential work of cultural discernment. Rather, it gives us hope for the long and patient task.

This leads to the first foundational practice for cultural engagement: *hosting*. By hosting, I mean first the way that living things "host" a viral

strain. This testifies to the way that the Word of God, coming from without, seeks to work its way in, to the most "inward parts" of a culture.
Dutch missiologist J. H. Bavinck (nephew of Herman Bavinck) described
it this way:

> The Christian life does not accommodate or adapt itself to heathen forms
> of life, but it takes the latter in possession and thereby makes them new.
> . . . The Christian life takes them in hand and turns them in an entirely
> different direction; they acquire an entirely different content. . . . Christ
> takes the life of a people in his hands, he renews and re-establishes the
> distorted and deteriorated; he fills each thing, each word, and each practice
> with a new meaning and gives it a new direction. Such is neither "adap-
> tion" nor accommodation; it is in essence the legitimate taking possession
> of something by him to whom all power is given in heaven and on earth.[25]

Even as every culture can host the gospel, theology seeks to "host" the
infections of gospel and culture, believing that ultimately the good infection will triumph over all our diseases.

When it comes to the practice of hosting itself, I have in mind the
more ordinary use of the word: the practice of hospitality, of "making
room" for others.[26] Following the example of Jesus, theology welcomes
all parties to the table who are willing to sit down for a meal. But it
seeks to remind the other parties not to dominate the conversation.
Life always takes place before the face of God, and theology seeks to
remind all those at the table that the most important voice to hear is the
voice of God. For whether we like it or not, there is no other table than
the one at which God is present. God is the transcendent Other, whose
presence is gift, begotten not made, always arriving from the outside
of every culture. Jesus embodies this role beautifully, transforming the
role of guest and offering himself to us as *the* host in his Holy Supper.
Thus, even as theology seeks to host culture, it also reminds us that *we*
always remain the guests of Jesus.

It can be tempting for Christians to revert to thinking of "the culture" as contagion—intrinsically harmful to human flourishing—as if
we could extract ourselves from "the culture" into a purely "biblical"
way of life. But such an extraction is neither possible nor desirable. What
is possible, though, is to strengthen our powers of discernment so that
our cultural immune systems are more consonant with a biblical vision

of human flourishing. This, of course, is easier said than done. For what we find is that the malignancy of sin is incredibly resilient, corrupting human hierarchies, not just human hearts. That is to say, culture is not just about meaning; it is also about power. And power has a way of exploiting the imbalances among the guests, shifting the way that theology "hosts." To that topic we now turn.

Questions for Reflection and Discussion

1. This chapter offered multiple images and analogies for culture and the gospel: virus, immune system, bubble, web, infection, host. Which of the images do you find most helpful? Which images are the most limited or misleading? What other images might be fruitful?

2. How does thinking about culture through the biblical patterns of ecosystem/exile, purity/pollution, and Spirit/community open up the conversation between theology and culture?

3. What differences result from treating holiness as something fragile to be protected versus treating it as something powerful to be unleashed?

4. How can Christians cultivate a thick community, one that both wrestles with the cost of discipleship and is hospitable and welcoming toward outsiders?

5. What does the foundational practice of "hosting" cultural voices, artifacts, and movements look like in everyday life? What are the possibilities and pitfalls of hosting?

THE POWER DIMENSION

Culture as Power Play

One of the first times that I had the opportunity to give a lecture in graduate school, I was asked to survey approaches to cultural engagement. I concluded my lecture with something like the twin axioms from the previous chapter: every culture is an adequate host for the gospel, and the gospel calls every culture to repentance. It was the first axiom that produced an objection. A student gingerly raised his hand and asked, "What about the Nazis?"

At this point it is instructive to bring up Godwin's Law of Nazi Analogies. In the days when the internet was young, early adopter Mike Godwin observed how frequently the Nazis were invoked in online discussions. Believing that such quick analogies "trivialized the horror of the Holocaust and the social pathology of the Nazis," he deployed a "counter-meme" to fight the infection. Godwin's Law maintains that the longer a debate goes on, the higher the probability that someone will compare the other side to Hitler or the Nazis.[1] Invoking Godwin's Law pushes back against such glib comparisons, exposing their real purpose: to villainize the opposition and "win" the conversation.

For the student in my lecture, however, it seemed that rather than trying to score a point, he was looking for the limits of cultural hospitality.

Absolute hospitality, after all, would welcome the devil himself.[2] Some cultural ideologies are demonic, and those who seek to destroy the other guests are not welcome at the table. Our tendency to bring up the Nazis exists in part because in them we find a seemingly unambiguous face for evil. The evils perpetrated by the Third Reich were horrific on an order of magnitude that prevents any cheap appeals for the sake of argument. Godwin's Law reminds us of our capacity for self-justification by comparison and of the temptation to vilify our critics. It is always easier to see evil in our enemies than in ourselves. But the point stands: radical evil exists, and it must be resisted. How do we distinguish it? And how shall we resist it?

Any discussion of theology and culture worth its salt must deal with the way that human creativity has been leveraged in service of idolatry and injustice. The vainglory and violence that result justly deserve condemnation, both human and divine (Rom. 3:8). Theology provides an incisive diagnosis of cultural pathologies (the pervasiveness of sin); more importantly, it points to a cure (God's redemptive intervention). But in the hands of fallen humans, theology has just as often been complicit in the pathologies, offering divine sanction to systemic evils, like race-based chattel slavery.[3]

This is one more reason why the conversation between theology and culture requires not just the discernment of spirits outside the walls of the church but also self-examination and repentance for what goes on within. Sin saturates our theologizing just as surely as it does our culture making. This does not mean that theology must remain silent. But it does shape the way theology speaks. For Christians, doctrines of sin *and* grace puncture our pride, preventing all self-congratulation. It leaves us even more desperate to hear a voice that comes from the outside, a voice that is radically Other, a voice that cannot be reduced to our own ingenuity (2 Pet. 1:16).

In the last chapter, I described culture as an immune system, an ecosystem of meaning that is hospitable to certain cultural strains and hostile to others. By choosing this metaphor, I have tried to capture the dynamic nature of culture, over against more inert metaphors (culture as text). We tend to describe cultures as if they were internally consistent, characterized by clear boundaries and broad consensus about the meaning of the world, as if "Christian culture," "campus culture," or "cancel culture" were singular things. But culture is always messy, and anyone on the inside of a culture is well acquainted with its nuance, diversity, and tensions. As a Christian, I often am embarrassed by the public figures who are thought to speak for my community, just as I am frustrated when my theological tradition is represented unfairly. I'm sure it is the same way for members of other groups, whose cultural distinctiveness appears uniform to outsiders.

The reality is that within every culture there is a struggle over whose perspective is normative and whose meaning matters the most. This chapter is concerned with that struggle for the center. My aim is to sketch an account of culture centered on the dynamics of power, in dialogue with the discipline usually employed for this task, critical theory. Although it is widespread in the mainstream academy, critical theory is regarded with deep suspicion—if not outright hostility—in some Christian circles. Some may consider my inclusion of this discipline to be problematic, in danger of compromising my entire project. But theology's complicity in cultural evil—its frequent inability to escape the pull of cultural pathologies—should make us all the more ready to listen to those who call us to account. Certain critical voices have not been fully heard, and so in this chapter we will engage in an exercise of inclusive listening. I will pay particular attention to the testimony of those who claim that culture is mostly about power.

"Testimony" is the right word, given that the lingering presence of injustice and abuse in our churches and communities puts us all in the dock. These critical witnesses are not our final judge, but neither are we ourselves. All human judgment is necessary but provisional, and the judge is Jesus Christ, "who will bring to light what is hidden in darkness and will expose the motives of the heart" (1 Cor. 4:5). It is in anticipation of that "day in court" that we should be willing to suffer the scrutiny of others as we wait (2 Tim. 1:12). This compels us to explore the basic framework of critical theory while also considering the way that theology offers a chastened way forward. The distinctive practice offered in this chapter will be iconoclasm, an act of naming and negating. Proper iconoclasm, I will argue, requires the calibration of our attention: we need to be able to see pathologies of power without allowing power to become the only thing we can see.

Critical Theories: Detecting Power Failures

Critical theory signifies a broad sensibility rather than a single intellectual stream. That sensibility aims to expose the way that culture perpetuates imbalances in power. It usually begins by pointing out disparities between various groups, which result in massive inequities not just in quality of life but also in quantity. If a global pandemic has exposed our shared vulnerability as creatures, it has also exposed the scandal of structural inequities (such as access to health care) that make some exceedingly more vulnerable than others.[4] The evidence of inequity is overwhelming. How do we account for it?

Modern critical theorists are hardly the first to reckon with this data. Consider the words of the Teacher in Ecclesiastes:

> Again I looked and saw all the oppression that was taking place under the sun:
>
>> I saw the tears of the oppressed—
>>   and they have no comforter;
>> power was on the side of their oppressors—
>>   and they have no comforter. (Eccles. 4:1)

While this led the Teacher to a sense of resignation—if not despair—most other biblical voices respond to the reality of oppression with calls for justice. This is the particular focus of the Hebrew prophets: calling God's people to covenant faithfulness means addressing "unjust laws" and "oppressive decrees" that "deprive the poor of their rights and withhold justice" from widows and orphans (Isa. 10:1–2). For the prophets, as long as injustice is allowed to continue, worship is compromised. In response to the scrupulous fasting of his people, God calls for a more holistic devotion:

> Is not this the kind of fasting I have chosen:
> to loose the chains of injustice
>   and untie the cords of the yoke,
> to set the oppressed free
>   and break every yoke? (Isa. 58:6)

The prophet Amos similarly thundered with a resounding anthem: "Let justice roll on like a river, righteousness like a never-failing stream!"

(Amos 5:24). Since justice and righteousness are aspects of God's character (Ps. 89:14), the call to address injustice is binding on all of God's creatures. This is especially incumbent on those with power, and so we find Daniel giving this counsel to the world's most powerful emperor: "Renounce your sins by doing what is right, and your wickedness by being kind to the oppressed" (Dan. 4:27).

On the surface, critical theories seem to work from a similar starting point as the Scriptures (recognition of oppression) and seek similar outcomes (justice). But as we dig deeper, we find significant differences in how oppression, liberation, and justice are defined, as well as in the story of the world that lies beneath these definitions. Part of the difficulty is that many critical theories employ a *methodological* naturalism (the commitment to empirical analysis) that is often paired with a *metaphysical* naturalism (the conviction that nothing supernatural exists). The former offers the hope of something like objectivity, because outcomes can be quantified, examined, and tested. But the latter entails a philosophical worldview without God, itself a faith commitment that is beyond the ability of empiricism to prove. As we examine critical theories, it is often difficult to discern where methodology ends and metaphysics begins. Perhaps this is unsurprising: neither our methods nor the ways we use them are neutral; they are always situated within a particular historical and cultural context. Furthermore, *all* claims about reality are funded by faith, unprovable assumptions about the nature of the world.[5] The idea of "secular justice" makes many Christians suspicious: these Christians consider such claims to be naive at best, malicious at worst. In varying degrees, they reject how critical theorists describe the nature and extent of oppression (the diagnosis), as well as what justice would look like in practice (the prescribed cure).

But perhaps it is possible to suspend judgment for the moment to describe the critical approach more fully. In practice, critical theory is a diagnostic tool calibrated to detect power imbalance in human society. We might say that what distinguishes critical theories from more traditional ones is an *activist* intent rather than a merely *interpretive* one. This follows Marx's famous dictum: "The philosophers have only *interpreted* the world in various ways; the point is, to *change* it."[6] Changing the world, in the critical tradition, means changing the social conditions that shape human consciousness. Critical theories are thus aimed at the structures of society, paying attention to power relations and seeking to unmask ideology (power masquerading as truth) in order to free humans from oppressive circumstances of all kinds. There are many critical approaches deployed by various disciplines (e.g., literary studies, legal studies) and organized around the interests of various groups (based on race, gender, sexual orientation, etc.). To take stock of all varieties of critical theory is far beyond the scope of this short chapter. Yet we can note the common concern to work against the pathologies of power and briefly survey this sort of analysis before seeking theology's contribution to these questions.

Classical Streams: Marx and the Frankfurt School

Where should we begin to unfold such an intricate tradition? Three figures loom large, the "masters of suspicion": Karl Marx (1818–1883), Friedrich Nietzsche (1844–1900), and Sigmund Freud (1856–1939). All three gave incisive critiques of dominant cultural norms. All three saw something hidden beneath claims of neutrality (economic oppression, the will to dominate, sexual desire). All three deeply influenced contemporary Western views of society and the self.[7]

In this chapter I can only discuss one of the three. I have chosen Marx, chiefly because his name comes up most frequently in everyday conversations (e.g., "cultural Marxism") in ways the others do not, even if their ideas have cast an equally long shadow. Despite the name recognition, however, the extent of most people's knowledge of Marx goes something like the conversation between two characters on the popular American sitcom *Parks and Recreation*:

> Ron Swanson: Libertarianism is all about individual liberty, and it should never be defined by the terms "liberal" or "conservative."
>
> Andy Dwyer: [Trying to contribute] And Communism . . . is no good.
>
> Ron Swanson: That's right. Big swing and a miss.[8]

The idea (at least for those who live in midwestern American communities like the one where the sitcom is set) is that Marxism has been totally discredited. Whether it is faulted for its atheistic presuppositions, economic determinism, utopian naivete, centralization of state power, or the tyranny and terror in Communist regimes, the verdict seems clear: Marx's project was a "big swing and a miss."[9] The Cold War is over; Marx and his minions lost.

But Marx's legacy is alive and well. Some of his hopes have been realized, integrated into Western cultural norms: the abolition of child labor and free public education, for example. Class consciousness and concern for social welfare have taken root in most Western societies, even if it did not require the abolition of private property, as Marx imagined. Nevertheless, Marx's dreams of social utopia and failed attempts to realize them have produced a fierce resistance in many cultural immune systems wherein social*ism* is synonymous with the loss of individual freedom. Among some Christians, "Marxist" is a label that confers guilt by association. There is a troubling tendency to categorize *any* discussion of power imbalance as covertly "Marxist" to dispose of it more easily. The result is that few Christians have taken time to hear the complaint of Marx and his heirs, who are often quite critical of Marx himself.

Marx's project is an economic critique, where capitalism is the Big Bad. "The history of all previously existing society," he famously wrote, "is the history of class struggles."[10] This struggle was chillingly concrete for Marx, evident in the ongoing dehumanization of workers in the industrial age. Imagine your children working long hours in a factory, and you begin to feel the force of the critique. The strong have always dominated the weak in this way, Marx believed, and they would continue to do so until the oppressed united to overthrow their oppressors. In this account, *economics determines culture*. Marxist cultural analysis highlights the ways that the powerful ensure they will remain in power. Since economic agency is the most important variable, strength is signified by securing the means of production: possessing the land, factory, and machinery; setting wages and underpaying workers; adding value to products that never benefit the laborers. For Marx, this economic struggle orients the entirety of human experience.[11]

Marx's sensitivity to power imbalance has blossomed in all sorts of unanticipated iterations. Often these critiques work from an atheistic starting point, following Marx himself. Some are openly hostile toward theology, believing with Italian neo-Marxist Antonio Gramsci (1891–

1937) that "socialism is precisely the religion that must kill Christianity."[12] Other times, Marxist analysis has been replanted in more transcendent soil, as with the "liberation theology" movement that began in Latin America in the latter half of the twentieth century.[13] These distinctions matter, and we must be careful not to paint every critique of power with an overbroad brush.

It seems to me that Marx's obsessive focus on class caused him to oversimplify, if not mistake, the relationship of culture and economics. His hostility to Christianity notwithstanding, Gramsci's analysis was closer to the mark: culture and economics are always mutually shaping. Economic policy in general (and capitalism in particular) evolves and is embedded in cultural institutions, especially the creative institutions that help us make meaning. These institutions must be transformed themselves if there is to be a meaningful change in material conditions. This is one reason why Marx's inevitable revolution did not occur, at least not as he imagined it.

Insight into the interdependence of culture, capital, and power is also reflected in the neo-Marxist group known as the Frankfurt school, most notably in the work of Max Horkheimer (1895–1973), who coined the term "critical theory."[14] Invoking Hitler was justified in the case of these thinkers, most of whom were also Jewish. They fled fascist regimes as the Nazis ascended to power, and some, like Walter Benjamin, did not escape. In exile, they wrote incisively about the relationship of culture and control, focusing on the way "culture industries" churn out media for the masses: movies, television, novels, theme parks, and sporting events. These spectacles offer modern versions of the Roman Empire's "bread and circuses," perpetuating cultural ideologies, justifying the way things are, distracting us from the reality of injustice. Political and economic freedom are increasingly curtailed, exchanged for a false freedom of choice among countless consumer products.[15] Although these diversions grant us some level of escape, it is a relief that fails to make a material difference. A family may have a Netflix subscription, an Xbox, and access to endless online content, but never be able to access healthy food options, save for retirement, or transfer wealth to the next generation.

This does not mean that ordinary people are helpless to resist. Countercultural movements, nonconforming subcultures, and resistance art emerge in opposition to mass culture's decadence and discrimination.

We might think of the role of rock and roll in the 1960s, or the golden age of hip-hop in the 1980s and '90s. And yet, culture industries work tirelessly to appropriate and incorporate the dissent of subcultures that would otherwise overturn the status quo. Resistance art loses its potency, either by "selling out" or by being drowned out as one more consumer option. Replacing religion, popular culture has become the new opiate for the masses, a primary means by which the elite preserve their privilege. For the Frankfurt school, as for Marx, the most important variable to consider when analyzing culture is power imbalance, the way culture's distinctions, divisions, and distractions serve the interests of those nearer to the center, at the expense of the vulnerable, who have been pushed to the margins.

Contemporary Conversations: Critical Race Theory and Black Lives Matter

My goal is not to sketch a comprehensive picture of critical theory in all its variety, still less to offer a satisfying refutation. The truth is that its sprawling diversity makes critical theory slippery to define and engage. I simply want to note that attention to power imbalance dominates contemporary discussions of culture, provoking an allergic reaction in many Christian communities. In some circles, the critical sensibility is rejected outrightly: its detractors argue that critical theorists work from assumptions—such as the plasticity of human nature and the rejection of biblical norms—that are in opposition to the scriptural account of flourishing. Rather than exposing the pretensions of the powerful, critical theory entails the enshrinement of a rival worldview—if not a rival religion. This leads some to turn the tables, claiming that critical theories are themselves power plays from secular elites. In their revolutionary zeal, they inevitably overcorrect, overturning societal order and harming ordinary people.[16] Given these fears, it is tempting to keep discussions of power dynamics at arm's length.

But the power critique is a perspective that Christians—especially those in dominant groups—must take time to hear. Arguments about methods matter, but they must not divert us from attending to abuses of power and the ongoing harm to our fellow image bearers, especially the vulnerable members of our families, churches, and communities. These wounded image bearers speak to us in prophetic voices, signifying in large, flashing letters, "THINGS ARE NOT RIGHT."[17]

Consider the examples of critical race theory (CRT) and Black Lives Matter (BLM). Both movements are quite controversial, especially among white Christians. Both acronyms are in danger of becoming "empty signifiers," vague references that absorb whatever meaning observers impose upon them (like an inkblot test). But this has not always been the case. CRT began as a legal movement interested in empirical evidence of racial inequity, seeking to answer the question, Did the reforms of the civil rights movement actually result in justice for Black Americans? Critical race theorists argue that there is an ideology of white supremacy enshrined in our institutions, which works against our best intentions to judge each person not "by the color of their skin but by the content of their character." We may pretend to be "color-blind," but this assumes that a person's appearance has no bearing on how they are treated by others in a racialized society. CRT argues that a level playing field does not actually exist and that this can be demonstrated empirically.[18] On a parallel track, the continuing pattern of police officers killing unarmed Black image bearers has resulted in widespread protests and the Black Lives Matter movement. When it comes to BLM, we are again referring to a sensibility rather than a single stream. The ubiquitous, untrademarked phrase or hashtag (#BLM) is the most visible symbol of a larger, decentralized movement advocating for racial justice, one that includes multiple organizations, chapters, and groups throughout the United States.

A common accusation is that both CRT and BLM represent the political agenda of "cultural Marxism," one that divides society into the oppressors and the oppressed, distinguishes between the racists and the anti-racists, and seeks to turn the underdogs into overlords.[19] Ironically, much of the energy in the debates is spent on whether we can categorize these movements as Marxist, as if that is all we need to know. Indeed, when a video circulated in which leaders of a prominent BLM organization identified themselves as "trained Marxists," that was enough for some not only to disqualify the entire movement but to refrain from uttering the words "Black lives matter." To speak these words is not an assertion of solidarity and Black dignity but a cultural shibboleth and capitulation to an atheistic agenda.

It seems to me that these discussions too often bury the lede. In both CRT and BLM, we find strains of resistance whose proponents start, not with Marx, but with their own experience of race-based discrimination (which in many cases they also seek to show empirically).[20] For Christians, experience and empirical evidence are both legitimate sources, even if they are not our final source. Like every source, they must be tested in light of what we find in Scripture. Thus, when confronted with the testimony of Black brothers and sisters, in which direction does Scripture lead? Does it lead us first to affirm the preciousness of every Black life, and to weep with those who weep, or does it lead us first to criticize the ideological framework of the protest? It is possible to do both: to defend dignity while discerning ideology. But there should be no confusion as to which should be the primary claim and which should be the footnote.

Indeed, Black Christians often remind their critics that they do not need a nineteenth-century German philosopher to tell the story of their own oppression. Furthermore, *they* at least are drawing not from Marxist sources but from biblical ones: the Hebrew prophets, Jesus, and Paul.[21] This does not mean that they are right about everything or that they are right by virtue of the evil that has been perpetrated against them. But they are telling the truth about their experiences. And they are using arguments from Scripture to call the broader church to greater faithfulness. This testimony must be heard, especially by Christians who believe that every Black life is an irreplaceable image of God.

When it comes to critiques of power dynamics within a cultural setting—whether they are centered in discussions of race, gender, or any other variable—our starting point should not be tracing the provenance (does it come from Marx?) or unveiling the metaphysical presuppositions (is it atheistic?). It is rather to recognize the dignity of our fellow human beings and to recognize when their dignity is being violated.[22] It is to be humbled by the pervasive prevalence of injustice, not just in individual attitudes but in institutional structures. This means seeing and taking seriously the undeniable suffering of groups who have been disinherited, denied the dignity that is theirs by virtue of being image bearers. It means being broken open, suffering silent humiliation, and putting our defensiveness to death—at least for a time (three days?). Only then are we prepared to speak.

Chastening Theory and Theology

Theology requires us both to describe the world and to seek to change it where we can. And though we should be slow to speak, especially where the suffering of others is concerned, after long listening a response is required (James 1:19). Loving the Lord our God requires us also to love our neighbor as ourselves, and this means defending their dignity while resisting their dehumanization (Luke 10:25–37). This is the particular responsibility of those who find themselves with cultural power. In the words of King Lemuel's mother,

> Speak up for those who cannot speak for themselves,
>   for the rights of all who are destitute.
> Speak up and judge fairly;
>   defend the rights of the poor and needy. (Prov. 31:8–9)

Scripture has nothing but strong words for those who lay oppressive burdens on others but refuse to lend a hand (Matt. 23:4). To call for justice in the church and in the wider culture is properly theological speech, rooted in doctrines like the character of God, the image of God, and the hope of God's coming kingdom.

But theology also means contending for the faith that has been entrusted to us (Jude 3), seeking to discern how hospitable cultural accounts might be to the vision of human flourishing we find in Scripture. How, then, might we begin to evaluate critical theory? We can affirm the concern for the marginalized, and the desire for justice, but we must also seek better soil in which to plant these impulses. At the height of the Cold War, Martin Luther King Jr. called Communism a "Christian heresy." Heresies always take some true element of the Christian story and blow it up at the expense of the larger picture. Communism is a *heresy*, King argued, because in its humanism it believes that "man, unaided by any divine power, can save himself and usher in a new society." But it is a *Christian* heresy because Marx took hold of something that was deeply Christian—"a protest against the injustice and indignities inflicted upon the underprivileged"—and extracted it from the larger story in which such a protest becomes sustainable.[23] Without the larger story, its vision of justice will always be incomplete.

What is that larger story? I have always appreciated the summary given by ethicist Lewis Smedes:

1. In the beginning, God made the world wonderfully good.
2. Near the start, the human family brought evil into the world's awesome goodness.
3. In the end, God will come to fix his world and make it altogether good again.
4. In between, his children are to go into the world and create some imperfect models of the good world to come.[24]

Smedes reminds us that evil is a human contribution, and that injustice is rooted in human rebellion, rather than in the structure of God's good creation. Furthermore, the healing of creation is possible first through divine intervention, and only secondarily through human participation. This means that our efforts matter, but that our efforts are not ultimate. It is not optional for Christians to be concerned for justice. But even as we work for justice, we remember that the ultimate hope of the weak, the hungry, the poor, and the dead is not in audacious human projects to fix the planet. Our hope, and the hope of all oppressed people living on the margins, is the kind of God our God is: one who brings reversal, setting disordered things in order again.[25] We can see this in the song of Hannah in the Old Testament and the song of Mary in the New (1 Sam. 2:1–10; Luke 1:46–55). It is precisely because God is engaged in this kind of project that *our* efforts are not in vain. It is precisely because his is the kingdom where there will be no injustice that we can put our hands to that task now. It is precisely because he is bringing a kingdom where justice rolls down that we can put our hearts to that task now.

The problem with our "imperfect models" is that we often underestimate just how thoroughly sin saturates everything we do: our institutions as well as the intuitions they form. Critical theory and Christian theology are both subject to self-deception, which is why we must insist on subjecting both to critique, always seeking to be reformed by the Word of God. For although the gospel is not a fragile thing to be contained, our cultural translations of the gospel can feel fragile, always subject to misinterpretation. When the gospel meets culture, it always takes root in cultural soil. The danger is that as faith and culture mix, we will mistake one for the other. Mixing the two is unavoidable; it is simply part of being human. But *mistaking* the two—taking cultural norms as theological nonnegotiables—is syncretism.

It is always easier to see syncretism in someone else's faith than in our own. It is easier for Christian conservatives to see cultural capitulation among progressives in sexual norms and for Christian progressives to see cultural captivity among conservatives when it comes to nationalism. It is always easier to see how culture situates the way someone else sees the world than to examine our own cultural lenses. One of the reasons we need critiques from the margins and from outsiders is because as insiders we often fail to see just how imperfect our models are. We realize this anytime we are released from our cultural echo chambers. Reading the accounts of believers from other centuries can free us of our chronological snobbery, just as meeting believers from other parts of the world can help Western believers see how deeply consumerism and celebrity have saturated our faith. No matter where or when we live, we can become overly attached to cultural expressions of Christianity, overvaluing them, idolizing them, unaware of how they disenfranchise those who are not like us.

At the same time, critical theories must also be chastened by the Word of God. Within critical accounts we find the temptation to collapse *everything* into power dynamics, and to insist that all claims of normativity or creational order are intrinsically violent, thinly veiled power plays. Critical theory becomes reductionistic when it abstracts coercive power as *the* aspect that determines all other aspects of reality. When this is the only lens we have for cultural interpretation, it is unsurprising that power becomes the only thing we ever see. As the saying goes, when you have a hammer, everything looks like a nail.

Yet there are a lot of nails, so to speak, and we are more likely to notice them when we suffer power's abuse. So how do we learn to see power as an important aspect of culture yet refuse to let it overpower our lived interpretations? Let us explore two theological threads that can help us think about the power dimension in culture: identification (naming, a political act) and iconoclasm (negating, a purgative act).

Theological Thread 1: Identification—Naming as Political Act

Meaning making always has a power dimension. An essential part of the "dominion" entrusted to humanity in the early pages of Scripture is the power to name the world: "Whatever the man called each living creature, that was its name" (Gen. 2:19). Naming here represents the attempt to find a connection between the sound of the word and the sense of where each named thing fits in the world. As Hans Rookmaaker puts it, "The uniqueness of [humanity's] relationship to both God and the world is at once apparent in the name-giving with which man started his activities, for giving a name is more than just labeling things in an arbitrary way. It means ordering, finding relationships, and perceiving individual qualities. It means discovering, not inventing (for man does not really invent anything), what the created world in its inexhaustible multiformity and variety has to offer."[26] *Discerning* is preferable to Rookmaaker's language of *discovering*, not least because of how "doctrines of discovery" have been deployed.[27] But the larger point stands: original power is fundamentally the exercise of creativity, and this power exists for the sake of the flourishing of creation. Naming is an exercise not of raw power that *confers* identity but of creative agency that *discerns* identity among ordered relationships.[28] Prior to humanity's estrangement from God, there is a sense of harmony between the world and the way humans name it. The world yields itself to humanity for naming, just as the ground offers itself for gardening. To name the world is to tell the truth about it, as carefully and clearly as we can.

But outside Eden, the task of naming becomes fraught with trouble. The creational call for loving dominion gives way to a sinful lust for domination. Creativity gives way to coercion. Rather than seeking lovingly to unfold the potencies of creation, we use our words in service of our own survival and success, seeking power *over* other image bearers. We cannot help but name the world. But our naming often only captures our own self-serving perspective, failing to discern right relationships within the created order. Apart from divine intervention, we name the world as those estranged from the God whose creational intent gives our meaning its ground and coherence with reality.

Indeed, now a malignancy has been unleashed in the world. The first time the word "sin" is mentioned in the biblical text, it is described like a wild animal, ready to devour Cain as he contemplates violence against his brother Abel: "Sin is crouching at your door; it desires to have you" (Gen. 4:7). After fleeing God's presence, Cain builds a city and names it after his son Enoch. This is significant because outside of Eden, his son now represents the only possibility of immortality—the survival of his line. For his great-great-grandson Lamech, this commitment to survival will grow into something more: a desire to dominate. Lamech is the first man in Scripture who takes multiple wives; he is remembered for his song about the new dog-eat-dog world: "I have killed a man for wounding me" (4:23). The impulse not simply to survive but to dominate is writ large several chapters later with the tower builders of Babel, who leverage their cultural power to "make a name" for themselves (11:4). As they do so, they imagine God is like them, in need of human-made stairs to climb down. They turn the Creator into a local deity, who gives sanction to their self-aggrandizement and sameness. It is because God loves his world that he frustrates this concentration of evil and the violent possibilities it could otherwise unleash. Judgment falls on human words, confusing their languages, and scattering them.

The confusion—intended as both judgment and mercy—remains with us in a multilingual, multicultural world. As a resident of the midwestern United States with dark hair and brown skin, I can't count the number of times I've been asked some version of the question, "Where are you from?" (Kansas!) or even more explicitly, "What are you?" (human!). I take these questions to be primarily a matter of curiosity, a desire to place me, even to hear a bit of my story. But when you are repeatedly asked these questions wherever you go, you begin to get the sense that although you are welcomed, you are still counted as an outsider, someone who is "not from here."

These smaller slights are given out of ignorance rather than malice. But it is also the case that those who consider themselves to be insiders (closer to the center of power) often use their words to reinscribe the lines of belonging. There is clearly a battle over how we name the world (e.g., What pronouns should we use? Should our politicians say "illegal immigrant" or "undocumented person"?). All words have histories, and meaning is constantly updated by use. Certain words and names should *never* be spoken—even in playful jest—because of the way they have been used to demean, degrade, and dehumanize image bearers.

This history should humble us. It testifies to the way that we have misused our power as stewards of creation in the attempt to be petty sovereigns, wannabe rulers accountable to no one but ourselves. It is no surprise that human culture from the time of Cain and Lamech is characterized by taking, killing, and empire building. Nor is it a surprise that naming becomes an exercise of raw power, either of self-assertion or domination. In a fallen world, we feel the truth of Michel Foucault's statement that culture often consists of "dividing practices" (stigmatizing and separating outcasts in hospitals, asylums, and prisons)[29] and that we often name the world to enshrine particular cultural traits (my food is normal; your food is "ethnic"). Too often our dividing practices are irrefutably insidious, such as the historic practice of "redlining," whereby the Federal Housing Administration refused to insure mortgages for Black Americans even as it subsidized intentionally segregated subdivisions for whites.[30]

Nevertheless, the whole of human life consists of more than dividing practices, more than oppression and subversion. The desire to dominate may situate our meaning making, but (against the masters of suspicion) it is not the sum of human desire. There are more dimensions of life than the political, and we can see the range of this as we consider the way naming works in the pages of the Bible. Naming is primarily conceived of as a way of making sense of experience, as in the forty or so instances in the Bible where a child is named to express gratitude, hope, or some other circumstance attending birth. Naomi, bereaved of husband and sons, renames herself Mara because of the bitterness that has befallen her (Ruth 1:20). Other times in Scripture, having multiple names is the result of inhabiting multiple cultural spaces (e.g., James/Jacob, Tabitha/Dorcas). And then there are the names given by conquerors to the conquered, as when Daniel, Hananiah, Mishael, and Azariah are carried into exile by the Babylonians, and as part of a forced cultural assimilation are renamed Belteshazzar, Shadrach, Meshach, and Abednego (Dan. 1:7).[31] And yet, even as these characters are in danger of losing their cultural and religious identity, they assert their agency in resisting the logic of the empire.

I want to make this point carefully, aware that most of the biblical documents were composed and compiled from the perspective of those living under various imperial occupations (e.g., Babylonian, Persian, Greek, Roman). The very act of telling the world's true story is a subversive act of resisting the pretensions of those who appear to hold all the power. Indeed, when names come from those who are on the underside of power, we should pay attention. Naming is a power that is in the hands of those who are in a culture's center, but it can also be in the hands of those who have been pushed to the margins. Historian Jemar Tisby demonstrates this as he advocates for the capitalization of the word "Black": "For generations, *Black* people have been denied the power of naming themselves, of self-identifying according to their history, heritage, and personality. Capitalizing the *B* in *Black* is an act of reclamation and dignity."[32] Tisby's call for capitalization shows the way that grammar in language shapes the "grammar" of our common life, the rules by which we navigate a world of divergent interests.

And yet, the most important names are never the ones conferred by those in power. Nor are they even the identities that we take up for ourselves to assert our agency and resist assimilation. The most important names are the ones offered to us by God. The most important perspective that Scripture has to give us on the power of names comes from those parts of the story where God steps in to offer a new name. Here we could mention Abram (renamed Abraham), Sarai (renamed Sarah), or Jacob (renamed Israel). We can also consider the promise of the prophet Isaiah to the inhabitants of Jerusalem:

> You will be called by a new name,
>   which the LORD's own mouth will determine.
> You will be a splendid garland in the LORD's hand,
>   a royal turban in the palm of God's hand.
> You will no longer be called Abandoned,
>   and your land will no longer be called Deserted.
> Instead, you will be called My Delight Is in Her,
>   and your land, Married.
> Because the LORD delights in you,
>   your land will be cared for once again. (Isa. 62:2–4 CEB)

Similarly, Paul tells the Galatians, "All of you who were baptized into Christ have clothed yourselves with Christ. There is neither Jew nor Gentile, neither slave nor free, nor is there male and female, for you are all one in Christ Jesus" (Gal. 3:27–28). Being "clothed" with Christ does not rewrite our prior history or remove all markers of difference. Rather, it bestows a new primary identity, reconfiguring our relationships, especially where power differentials exist.

A new name signifies the hope of a new future, new possibilities, and an identity that is neither an achievement by the powerful nor an act of self-assertion by the oppressed. It is an identity received as a gift, one that calls into question the names given to us by others, as well as the names that we take up for ourselves. It is altogether fitting that people self-identify, naming their own experiences with the language that is available to them. But these names are not fixed simply because we find them to be resonant. All the identities we own must find their ultimacy in response to the names offered to us by God. The names we give ourselves may be descriptively accurate in our cultural setting, but they are also provisional, open to the possibility of divine intervention and surprise. In her despair, Naomi wishes to be renamed; but the God of Israel had other plans. Her bitter self-identification is a moment that is heard, recorded, and taken seriously. But it is not definitive, because God reserves the right to enter and redeem her story in an unexpected way, through Ruth, the Moabite outsider.

The fact that the ultimate power to bestow identity rests with God means that it does not belong to any one culture, nation, or group. And yet we have at times so thoroughly mixed Christian faith with culture that we are unable to tell the difference. The confusion led well-meaning Christians, upon entering new lands, to seek to replace foreign cultural sensibilities with their own. As Willie Jennings writes, "Indeed, it is as though Christianity, wherever it went in the modern colonies, inverted its sense of hospitality. It claimed to be the host, the owner of the spaces it entered, and demanded native peoples enter its cultural logics, its ways of being in the world, and its conceptualities." This stands in stark contrast to the posture of "the Son of God, who took on the life of the creature, a life of joining, belonging, connection, and intimacy."[33] We should lament how often Christians—in positions of privilege and power—have set themselves in God's place, taking for themselves the right to give the *final* names to their fellow image bearers. This is a matter not just of injustice but of idolatry. And idolatry calls for iconoclasm.

Theological Thread 2: Iconoclasm—Negating as Purgative Act

Iconoclasm has traditionally held an explicitly religious meaning, referring to the rejection or removal of images in worship. Following the first two commandments, it rejects all false gods in light of the revelation of the true God at Sinai (Exod. 20:2). But in the modern world, iconoclasm has broadened to include challenges against cherished icons or institutions in general. When we call someone an iconoclast, we mean a person who is unafraid to criticize society's "sacred cows." In a manner consonant with critical theory, the iconoclastic impulse seeks to unmask the pretensions of power, removing it from its pedestal, negating its legitimacy.

Indeed, iconoclasm has arguably become one of the most religious features of our secular age. The most common targets are icons associated with ideologies of violence. Sometimes religious symbols themselves are in view, as when the French government sought to diminish religious violence through forbidding religious apparel (headscarves, yarmulkes, crucifixes) in public schools.[34] More often, iconoclasts call out cultural symbols connected with legacies of oppression. This iconoclastic impulse reached critical mass after the murder of George Floyd in 2020. Protests around the world resulted in the pulling down of statues of slaveholders and the renaming of streets and schools. More everyday iconoclasm takes the form of "cancel culture," which seeks to deplatform public figures (past or present) because of their sins (past or present). These sins are almost always related to the abuse of power and privilege, either real or imagined.

My goal is not to adjudicate the legitimacy of these new strains of iconoclasm. Rather, it is to point out their fundamentally religious character, and their purgative (rather than purely destructive) aim. Iconoclasm seeks to cleanse the cultural imagination from the defilement of abuse. This has always been the case. When the Reformers sought to remove religious images in the sixteenth century, they were challenging those images' claim that God was present in *just this place*, leaving divine grace open to human manipulation and control. By removing images from their churches, the Reformers proclaimed a new understanding of God's presence in the wider world, the theater of God's glory. Theologian Natalie Carnes points out a similar dynamic at work in political revolutions: "The revolutionaries break images to repudiate the presence to which the images attest, and yet they break to proclaim—to prove—a new presence and power."[35] The problem is that new images become new idols, and the old iconoclasts become the new iconophiles. Statues are torn down, replaced with social media selfies, testifying to membership on "the right side of history." Old icons are canceled, and new exemplars are placed on pedestals. The imaginative vacuum aches to be filled, and new powers yearn to fill it. It is not for nothing that Calvin called the human heart a "factory of idols."[36]

Throughout Scripture the proscription of images (e.g., Exod. 20:4) seeks to protect humans from being shattered at the altars of our idols, because idolatry and injustice always go hand in hand.[37] Since humans are made in the image of God, they are regal, and they are responsible. The reduction of God to a lifeless idol accompanies the distortion of image bearers in becoming oppressors and the destruction of image bearers as they are oppressed. For this reason, reverence for God should make us loath to participate in anything that dishonors those who bear his image: "Whoever oppresses the poor shows contempt for their Maker" (Prov. 14:31).

Distinctive Practice: Iconoclasm

It is because of our idol-making tendency that some form of iconoclasm is necessary, and this is the distinctive interpretive practice for engaging the power dimension. Iconoclasm seeks to name and negate the pretensions of power whereby we make idols and break image bearers. Here it is important that we first look to ourselves, calling out the idols of our own communities before addressing the idols of those on the outside (Matt. 7:3). If we look closely, we will find that idols and ideologies also go together. Political theorist David Koyzis shows, for example, how political visions that include allegiance to an ideal are always in danger of becoming idols: liberalism (the individual), conservatism (the past), progressivism (the future), democratism (majority rule), or socialism (common ownership).[38]

Iconoclasm is thus a purgative practice whereby we subject our cultural values, political visions, and societal institutions to the good infection of the gospel, seeking to hear the voice that calls us to repentance and obedience. There are some cultural stories that will need to be replaced. But no culture is so fallen that *all* its stories need to be replaced. Some stories glimmer with common grace, and the gospel can complete them, giving them full meaning and purpose.

Here we can learn from Carnes, who distinguishes between two kinds of iconoclasm. The first focuses on the falseness of the image and seeks to remove it and replace it. Let us call this the iconoclasm of *cancellation*. This is the iconoclasm of critical theory: not *x* but *y*. For example, "You think this is about morality, but really it is about power." The second focuses on the fullness of truth and seeks to place an image among the countertestimony of other images: *x* but also *y*. This second sort of iconoclasm brings a critique "not by *dis*placing but by *em*placing in an album of images." By surrounding the original image with other sketches, it seeks "to loosen the grip a particular picture has on our imagination."[39] Let us call this the iconoclasm of *complication*. Rather than allowing a "single story" to stand, this sort of iconoclasm complicates the narrative to continue a more nuanced conversation.[40] Applied to our metaphor of table fellowship, cancellation would mean removing abusive guests from their chairs, while complication would mean inviting a more diverse group of guests to the meal, allowing them to select the menu, the venue, and the seating arrangements.

Both forms of iconoclasm—cancellation and complication—are necessary and legitimate. When we engage in iconoclasm, we seek to discern which elements need to be displaced and which cultural elements need to be decentered. The danger of the first variety is that in its zeal to purge, it is prone to violence itself; the danger of the second variety is that as images abound, it becomes difficult to distinguish what is true amid the multitude of perspectives. Applying these forms of iconoclasm, whether in resisting deception or in testifying to truth, is a matter of careful discernment, one in which we should keep a watch on ourselves, lest we should also be tempted (Gal. 6:1). This is why, when we engage in the practice of iconoclasm, we need to start with the idols of our own community. If it feels that I have been harder in this chapter on those within the walls of the church than on those without, it is because I am seeking to practice what I preach. Because the truth is that I also am in danger of remaking God in my own image, rebranding the Creator of everything as a shrunken deity who is concerned only with the interests of my own inner circles.

The revelation of God in Jesus Christ is, after all, God's ultimate act of iconoclasm. Jesus brings a critique that originates from the outside (it is transcendent in source), but it does not remain on the outside. Critiques from outsiders, after all, are limited in their options. They either overwhelm by force—replacing insiders with outsiders—or they remain outside, tolerated but ignored, lonely voices in the wilderness. For a critique to transform, it must take root within a culture's soil. As Walter Brueggemann writes, "Without the Cross, prophetic imagination will likely be as strident and as destructive as that which it criticizes. The Cross is the assurance that effective prophetic criticism is done not by an outsider but always by one who must embrace the grief, enter into the death, and know the pain of the criticized one."[41] The cross is not the critique of an outsider but the critique of one intimately acquainted with the underside of power, one who has suffered evil's brutality. Even as it joins humanity in suffering, the cross also reveals and rejects human ultimacy. It exposes the artless conspiracy of religious, political, and demonic power, disarming them, making them the public spectacle (Col. 2:15). For when the powers have done their worst, when they have efficiently extinguished the life of God's Son, he rises. Sin has been condemned in his flesh (Rom. 8:3), and all other claims of ultimacy have been unmasked as illusions. Power dynamics may determine who lives and who dies. But when Jesus rises from the dead, it means that human power never has the last word. It can never be the most defining reality. There is something deeper and more definitive: grace.

How do we learn to see the pathologies of power dynamics without those pathologies becoming the only thing that we see? This is a critical question for continuing the conversation between theology and culture, and standing in the shadow of the cross is a good place to start. Indeed, we should be wary of those whose cultural critique is not accompanied by a willingness to "suffer with" those who mourn, whose words flow faster than their tears. For though we should not reduce all of culture to the power dimension, we should acknowledge that theological triage requires us to account for this dimension as early as we can. We must deal with power because love requires the use of power. And the proper use of power requires a moral vision, an account of order, righteousness, and goodness, which is the subject of my next chapter.

QUESTIONS FOR
REFLECTION AND DISCUSSION

1. What has been your experience with critical theories? How do you assess the strengths and weaknesses, the potential and the pitfalls of power critique? How do we learn to see power dynamics without letting those dynamics become the only thing we see?

2. How do you understand the relationship between identity and power? In what way is your identity the product of powerful institutions, individual choice, and/or divine intervention?

3. Where do you see injustice in the cultures or communities of which you are a part? How are the instances of injustice connected to idolatry?

4. Where do you find both types of iconoclasm at work in the world? What does the distinctive practice of idolatry critique look like in real life? What does it mean for you to challenge your own idols and the idols of your own group first, before addressing the idols of others?

5. How does Jesus's practice of table fellowship (an act of joining) connect to his practice of asking penetrating questions (an act of interrogation)? At what point should we move from sitting at the table to flipping the table?

THE ETHICAL DIMENSION

Culture as Moral Boundary

While I was writing this chapter, I traveled to another city to give a pair of lectures on a college campus. The campus was relatively empty, and my slowly moving car was conspicuous as I tried to find coffee early one morning. A security guard approached my car and asked me whether I had any reason to be there. I replied that I was there for a conference where I had been invited to speak. It was clear that this did not allay his suspicions, and after an extended, unpleasant interaction, he let me leave, though he also followed me at a distance when I returned with coffee.

The experience rattled me, enough to make me avoid driving around the campus for the remainder of the conference. On top of the ordinary indignation of not being trusted, I also felt the charged uncertainty that persons of color often experience in such an encounter. He was quick to assure me, "It's just about keeping the kids safe; that's all this is about," as if he were also hyperaware of how the interaction could be interpreted. As I ran the encounter through my mind again and again, I tried to put myself in his shoes. Perhaps the security guard was just doing his job, policing the boundaries, and keeping the campus community safe from strangers. Perhaps it was unpleasant for him as well. Perhaps I could have been more deferential. Perhaps I don't have all the information. Perhaps there are other factors that explain his heightened vigilance: his personal history, institutional policy, or a pattern of suspicious persons. But I have a personal history as well. And I am also hyperaware that throughout America "ordinary stops" have had devastating results, especially for Black men and women.[1] By contrast, I never felt unsafe during the interaction, though I certainly felt unwelcome and unwanted.

My goal is neither to give a definitive interpretation of the interaction nor to make a point about patterns of policing. It is rather to highlight the way that stories like this trigger our moral intuitions, even if our intuitions differ. Some will feel hot indignation on behalf of the person mistrusted, while others will feel the cold necessity of vigilant watchfulness on behalf of the guard. Most of us feel these judgments in our bodies before we begin to articulate them in our words, especially when we believe ourselves to have been wronged!

We make these judgments because we are moral beings who feel in our bones that some cultural practices and artifacts reflect a world that's "not the way it's supposed to be."[2] Some bits of culture, like a concert in a park, seem more "life-affirming" than others; they seek to make things better, while others, like propaganda or pornography, are part of the problem. But as soon as we begin to make such distinctions— not describing what *is* but making claims about what *ought* to be—we manifest a moral vision, one that tells us, for example, that it is *better* to value life and alleviate suffering.

The point is that cultural analysis cannot be extracted from moral sensibilities, and moral sensibilities cannot be separated from our culturally inflected vision of the world. Indeed, culture requires moral imagination, a sense of what is good for our common life and what righteousness requires. As G. K. Chesterton reminds us, both morality and art require "drawing the line somewhere."[3] What is good for our community? What do we owe each other? What boundaries do we need to flourish? And how do we relate to those outside the boundaries? Answering these questions has given birth to the broad tradition known as ethics.

The discipline of ethics pairs critical diagnoses with constructive prescriptions, seeking to cultivate flourishing communities. The ethical dimension is connected closely with the power dimension explored in the previous chapter, and I am hoping to distinguish them without dividing them. Since critiques of coercive power tend to emphasize deconstruction (and the divestment of power), often a *constructive* moral vision is lost. But some use of power is inevitable as humans build lives together, and this means the iconoclast's hammer must give way to a different sort of craftsmanship, one that seeks to forge artifacts, communities, and institutions marked by goodness. In this chapter I will explore the shape of this moral making, seeking to understand how the human hunger for *righteousness* works itself out in culture. After responding to the objection that righteousness is really about reputation, I will follow theological threads that connect our moral impulse to answerability (its source) and servanthood (its stewardship). The distinctive practice that will emerge is "organic servanthood," whereby we seek to leverage whatever power we are given to make space for the flourishing of others.

Varieties of Vision: Seeking a Source for Our Moral Intuitions

In our exploration of theology and culture thus far, we have already encountered numerous ethical imperatives. We *ought* to listen to those outside the walls of the church. We *should* be humbled when we examine abuses of power within. We *must* test all things and hold fast to what is good. These prescriptions should come as no surprise to Christians. We are called to derive our ethical vision from and to test all cultural artifacts, movements, and institutions by what we regard as the true story of the world found in Holy Scripture.

This is easier said than done, of course. Lived interpretations of Scripture vary widely, and proof texts can be found for almost anything we want to justify.[4] Our divergent interpretations are due in part to the diverse cultural environments in which we are embedded, environments that create varying tensions with biblical themes. Western culture, for example, resonates with some biblical perspectives on wealth (e.g., saving for the future) while resisting others (e.g., sacrificial giving to the poor). This does not mean, however, that all interpretations are of equal value. Some interpretations are more fitting than others, and for any theology to be Christian, it must remain rooted in the biblical story, rendering it, in the words of Stanley Grenz, "trinitarian in content, communitarian in focus, and eschatological in orientation."[5] Despite our interpretive differences, the Christian faith should manifest itself in moral communities with a family resemblance, bearing the fruit of the Spirit (Gal. 5:22–25).

Together we seek to make imperfect models of the now-and-not-yet kingdom, characterized by "righteousness, peace and joy in the Holy Spirit" (Rom. 14:17). The point at the moment is not to adjudicate which interpretations are the most "biblical" but to show that for Christians the criteria for making judgments are intrinsic to Scripture itself. All Christians must wrestle with the demands of a Scripture-shaped life. The moral vision that informs Christian community has a shared source, even if the contours of that vision are contested.

The modern world, however, has multiplied moral visions beyond traditional sources. Many of these visions carry forward the ghosts of the past, drawing from classical, Jewish, or Christian intuitions, while leaving behind an explicitly religious worldview. Religions disagree, after all, and religious codes are often discordant with contemporary sensibilities. This has led modern thinkers to seek accounts of morality that do not require a transcendent source. In the absence of divine commands, how can we delineate right from wrong? The three most common approaches center on the calculation of consequences (utilitarianism), the making of categorical judgments (deontology), and the development of character (virtue ethics). We can follow Nicholas Wolterstorff in identifying three corresponding conceptions of "the good life": a life that is existentially satisfying, a life that goes well for all, and a life that is well lived.[6]

A famous thought experiment invites us to imagine sitting behind the wheel of a runaway trolley car. The trolley is on the verge of hitting five workers, but on a separate track sits another worker. If you had the ability to turn the wheel and switch the tracks, causing the trolley to hit one worker rather than five, should you?[7] The impulse to say yes signifies a *consequentialist* sensibility: since fewer people will suffer, the decision to turn the wheel is justifiable. In this line of thought, our moral sensibilities reflect habits of moral calculation as we seek to maximize pleasure while minimizing pain. This requires us to reason together about what sorts of things will serve the general welfare, but the basic logic is clear: the rightness of an action, rule, or law is measured by the consequences, and those consequences are measured in terms of existential satisfaction for all involved.

But we also feel another intuition: that turning the trolley's wheel would be wrong regardless of how many lives it saves. Some things are *categorically* right or wrong. To quote Steve Rogers of *Avengers* movie fame,

"We don't trade lives." A more sophisticated articulation of this perspective comes from German philosopher Immanuel Kant (1724–1804), who maintained that there are "categorical imperatives," absolute duties that must be followed regardless of the results (e.g., "It is always wrong to take human life"). To be human is to be free, and we are free only if we act from duty (which for Kant reflects the demands of pure reason) rather than being driven by inclination, calculation, or circumstance. A variation on this theme comes from moral philosopher John Rawls.[8] Rawls asks us to imagine what sort of rules we would make if we did not know where we fall in society's hierarchies. Under such a "veil of ignorance," Rawls argues, we would strive to establish an ideal society that is equitable for all, rather than tilted toward particular groups. Indeed, the goal for Rawls, Kant, and other deontologists (the prefix "deon" means duty) is to establish a moral system that is driven by principle rather than dependent on subjective interest.

In recent years, there has also been a resurgence of virtue ethics, which focuses on the formation of *character*. Unlike universalizing deontologists, virtue ethicists are more attuned to the narrative shape of various moral communities. In other words, beneath prescriptions of moral behavior lies some account of purpose: what humans are for. As Alasdair MacIntyre writes, "I can only answer the question 'What am I to do?' if I can answer the prior question 'Of what story or stories do I find myself a part?'"[9] The primary criterion of virtue ethics is not consequentialist (Will it result in general welfare?), nor is it categorical (Is it my duty?). Rather, it is teleological: What kind of person am I to do this, and is this the sort of person I want to become? In both deontology and virtue ethics, a life that is well lived may not always produce positive feelings. Nevertheless, it is the best way to live.

A fourth approach should be added, along the lines of the power critique in the previous chapter. Critical ethical theories begin by rejecting the "objective observer" standpoint of traditional frameworks, instead taking their stand among, with, and for marginalized groups. Drawing attention to the ways that these groups have been stigmatized and scapegoated, these critical prescriptions seek to decenter those who have been in power and instead attend to the oppressed. Even as old moralities are called into question, new moralities are conceived, centered on grievance against and justice for marginalized groups. If the traditional systems placed heavier emphasis on *a life well lived*, critical theories place heavier emphasis on *how life actually goes*, especially for the downtrodden. Here we can recall Marx's emphasis on material conditions.

This brief survey highlights both the inevitability and the intricacy of the ethical dimension. Whether we work from a traditional, modern, or critical framework, we cannot avoid making moral judgments about what is good for humans. We may call these rules, mores, or community standards. Some may be officially encoded into law, others taken for granted as cultural norms. But all our judgments set boundaries, placing some closer to the center while leaving others on the margins, or even outside. In every culture (and subculture), some attitudes and behaviors are considered ordinary, mainstream, and acceptable, while others are considered strange, unorthodox, or deplorable. The result is that cultures always have insiders and outsiders (and a range of people in between). I mean this simply as a descriptive claim: I am not implying that insiders are necessarily more virtuous than outsiders or that the lines have been correctly drawn. I use this language to highlight the fact that boundaries are inevitable, that they have a moral edge, and that a person's lived experience changes in relationship to the boundary.

The drawing of ethical boundaries in every culture should be unsurprising. Our moral triggers are tripped every day as we navigate life with others. Have you ever had someone step in front of you in line? Or been cut off in traffic? Life becomes unlivable without the ability to recognize boundaries between what is good for our common life and what is not, between what is right and what is wrong. Injustice, deception, and darkness must be named and negated as best we can.

The problem is not in having boundary markers but in how we live together with those along the edges or on either side. Boundaries need not harden into binaries, where we vilify those on the other side (us vs. them). We might say that the test of the health of a culture is how it treats its vulnerable members, those who don't measure up to cultural standards, and how it makes room for those who don't seem to fit. But the Christian ethic goes beyond this, measuring the community's fidelity not just by how it treats those within but also by how it relates to those without, how it loves its enemies (Matt. 5:44–45). Nevertheless, the point stands: cultural appreciation, neighborly affection, hospitality to strangers, and enemy love all assume a boundary, even if it is one that can be crossed. These boundaries are marked by various sorts of difference, but they almost always develop moral edges: Who are the good people? What is a great country? Who is on the right side of history?

Moral Foundations Theory: Interrogating Our Moral Intuitions

To put it another way, all cultures are concerned with *righteousness*. Few have made this point as incisively as social psychologist Jonathan Haidt. Recall that Haidt argues for six innate moral intuitions, which provide universal foundations for the diverse moral matrices found throughout human cultures. For each pair, we resonate with the first and resist the second:

1. Care versus harm
2. Fairness versus cheating
3. Liberty versus oppression
4. Loyalty versus betrayal
5. Authority versus subversion
6. Sanctity versus degradation

In Haidt's account, these intuitions derive from adaptive challenges of living together in community. They are triggered by historic threats or opportunities in a group's common life, such as caring for vulnerable children, forming partnerships beyond family, negotiating hierarchies, and keeping oneself free from pathogens.[10]

Although these intuitions are universal, they are also unevenly distributed. Moral intuitions are held in tension with one another, and societies valorize particular intuitions over others. Haidt compares our moral intuitions to taste receptors and argues that moral palates within societies develop over time. Moral sense shifts with cultural difference and with the cultural stories we absorb ("bring honor to your family" vs. "be true to yourself"). Western societies, for example, have grown in compassion for animal suffering (maximizing "care") while diminishing in disgust for various forms of sexual activity (minimizing "sanctity").[11]

Let me pause for a moment to note that Haidt's Moral Foundations Theory does not require us to believe that morality is relative or that moral judgment is *merely* a matter of taste. But it does require us to resist "moral monism," the attempt to ground all of morality on a single principle (such as harm or fairness). Such a project, Haidt writes, would be comparable to a restaurant that seeks only to satisfy a single taste receptor, like a restaurant specializing in salt! Reductive moral palates produce cultures that are bitterly fundamentalistic, blandly inoffensive, or cloyingly sentimental. What Haidt is after is a more diverse moral palate and a more patient world. He especially wants us to appreciate which moral intuitions lie beneath the positions of our ideological adversaries. Indeed, his research indicates that while those who self-identify as "politically left" tend to maximize the first three foundations (care/harm, fairness/cheating, liberty/oppression), traditional morality rests on all six foundations, albeit at non-maximal levels. Citing concern for victims, progressives are more willing to sacrifice proportionality when it conflicts with their desire to fight oppression, while traditionalists are more willing to sacrifice care to satisfy the other moral intuitions.[12] The polarization that occurs in diverse societies reflects not the clashing of good against evil but competing conceptions of the good: divergent, deeply felt moral intuitions.

Do We Really Want to Be Better? Challenging the Righteous Mind

Moral Foundations Theory also undermines the assumption that righteousness preoccupies only "religious people." Indeed, it is not difficult to find examples of religious zeal consuming the officially irreligious. Dave Zahl calls this impulse "seculosity": religiosity directed toward earthly objects. The religiously affiliated and unaffiliated alike manifest fervor for many things: food and fitness, politics and public health, sexual expression and social justice. The problem, Zahl contends, is not that religion is on the wane but that we are more religious than ever, and about too many things. We are almost never *not* in church.[13] Western people may be less officially devout, but there is no shortage of fundamentalism about what it means to be a good human.

Morality seeks a stage, a place to perform public virtue. Similarly, seculosity only makes sense when framed by the reality of life in front of—and in constant comparison with—those around us. Whatever we call our efforts to become better humans, our quest for improvement craves recognition from others who can certify our legitimacy. In a media-amplified environment, we seek public approval in the form of views, likes, and follows, and we dread social media shame—or worse, cancellation. Given the ever-increasing time we spend in digital spaces, the jury rendering the verdict on our lives is only loosely connected to us (strangers on Twitter!), resulting in an ever-more-fragile sense of self.[14]

This social dimension of morality, in which we seek to justify ourselves to those around us, raises a key question: Do we want to *be* moral or just to *appear* moral? In other words, is culture more concerned with righteousness or with reputation, our efforts to satisfy the scrutiny of those around us? This conundrum is at least as old as Plato, who records his brother Glaucon in conversation with Socrates on this very issue. Glaucon imagines a man with a magic ring that allows him to become invisible. (Perhaps this sounds familiar to Tolkien fans.) If a man possessed such a ring, Glaucon asks, why wouldn't he do as he pleases? The implication is that humans only value justice and morality because they lack the ability to get away with injustice and immorality.[15] "Doing the right thing" is really the sophisticated management of our public reputation, a way we win honor and avoid shame from the groups in which we seek to belong. If this sounds compelling, you are not alone in thinking so. Haidt puts forth his theory of moral intuitions under the conviction that Glaucon is right and that our desire to belong shapes both the way we behave and the behaviors we approve or condemn in others.

Righteousness as reputation management also maps onto contemporary conversations about "virtue signaling." Virtue signaling is the name given to the practice of performing actions to display our righteousness to others in our community (including on digital platforms). Signaling is unavoidable at some level. All of us send signals in the subtext of our actions, giving those around us clues that communicate something about who we are. I may wear a freshly pressed shirt to communicate that I am "put together" or a blazer to show that I am professional. In some situations, signaling virtue can be strategically appropriate. I have a friend who volunteered with a Christian organization that ministered to sex workers on the streets of Chicago. All the lay volunteers wore clerical collars as they walked the streets. They did this because on the streets the collar, at least at that time, was a clear signal that someone was a safe person.

Virtue signaling becomes problematic, however, when it is *merely* performative. Rather than being a substantive expression of a deeper moral vision, it is satisfied with the self-congratulation of being perceived as good. Like wearing the appropriate jersey to a sporting event, virtue signaling can be a way of saying, "I'm on the right team." That "team" may not necessarily be the one that is substantively engaged with justice, but it may be the one that offers me self-justification, a way to feel that I am approved and that I should be included among the righteous.

This sort of signaling is easy to find in the world of social media, where the extent of our "slacktivism" may consist in changing a profile picture, sharing a post, or following a cause. As the unrelenting reminders of injustice overwhelm us through our myriad streams, all sorts of banal dilemmas emerge. How often should we change our profile pictures to show solidarity? If we post about one cause but not another, does it compromise our compassion? If we don't post anything, will our silence be interpreted as complicity? In a hyperconnected world, activism often seems less about justice and more about managing our "brand identity" as those who care about the right things, who are safely situated on the right side of history.

The right side of history: notice that this privileged location seeks righteousness in the judgments of future generations, who will evaluate us from their inevitable position of progress. In other words, we can escape the thinness of our moral judgments by adding the weight of some imagined community of the future. We assert our belonging in that moral majority, whom we assume will hold a slightly upgraded version of the same values we do. And perhaps, in the absence of a divine judge, the best we can do is to say something like the line from the musical *Hamilton*: "History has its eye on you."

Is Belonging Enough? Transcendent Triggers for Moral Judgments

But we *must* do better than this if there is a God in whom "we live and move and have our being" (Acts 17:28). Both Glaucon in ancient times and Haidt in contemporary times are astute observers of human psychology and culture, and we can feel the explanatory force of their arguments. And yet, their accounts are incomplete because they treat moral intuition without reference to God. They are guided by twin assumptions of *instrumentality* and *immanence*. Let me explain what I mean by these terms.

An *instrumental* account of cognition understands reason and intuition as tools we use to cope with and control an inhospitable world. This is unsurprising given the emphasis on survival and selection common to evolutionary accounts, where the development of every cultural practice must be understood in terms of how it aided the adaptive tasks of our ancestors. This seems especially fitting from the perspective of a technological age, in which education is increasingly oriented toward solving technical problems rather than finding ultimate truths. But as Alvin Plantinga has argued, on a purely naturalistic account there is no reason to conclude that our faculties are reliably aimed at truth at all. We would need to access the world only insofar as it concerns our survival.[16] There is also a larger point to be made: instrumentality cannot exhaust the human hunger for truth, the desire to look into the very heart of things, the impulse of interiority, and the desire for integrity, to *be* true, to have "truth in the inward parts" (Ps. 51:6 KJV). We want to get hold of reality, drink deeply from it, not just survive it. And there is a kind of knowing—non-instrumental and poetic—that seems necessary to access deeper layers of reality.

This brings us to the second assumption: *immanence*, which means that we seek to understand the world apart from a transcendent source. Though immanence is our contemporary presupposition, for most people, morality has been about more than just the survival of their group against others. What evolutionary accounts overlook is the fact that for most of human existence, moral intuitions have been triggered by the apprehension of an enchanted cosmos. For inhabitants of the premodern world, and for many today in the non-Western world, we share space with unseen agents to whom we seek to be rightly related: spirits, angels, demons, and gods. As cognitive scientists of religion have argued, we are "born believers" in these things; it is unbelief that must be taught.[17] Even for those of us who supposedly live in a "disenchanted" world, where the "immanent frame" blocks our view of the divine, we remain haunted by transcendence.[18]

It is for this reason—secularism notwithstanding—that most of the world remains connected to some type of religious faith, engaged in ritual practices that form them as moral agents. It is not simply that a shared apprehension of the spiritual binds culture together, though that is certainly the case. It is also that we feel ourselves addressed by and accountable to some ultimate reality. Indeed, as anthropologist Tanya Luhrmann has argued, prayer's most consequential feature may be "that God is a social relationship in the life of the person who prays."[19] Yes, we behave because we want to belong. But this includes—often supremely—belonging to God. For if there is a God who addresses humans, then there will be other ethical criteria that transcend the demands of my local community and culture. As C. S. Lewis puts it, "Does it not make a great difference whether I am, so to speak, the landlord of my own mind and body, or only a tenant, responsible to the real landlord? If someone made me, for his own purposes, then I shall have a lot of duties which I should not have had if I simply belonged to myself."[20]

Christian faith begins with the comfort and challenge that we are not our own; we belong to God. Since a culture's moral imagination can become diseased,[21] and moral frameworks often seek to justify the unjustifiable, there must be a deeper basis for solidarity and a higher court of appeal than my local belonging. This brings us, finally, to two theological threads that help us make sense of the ethical dimension of culture: (1) answerability and autonomy and (2) stewardship and servanthood.

Theological Thread 1: Answerability versus Autonomy

My argument is that our moral visions in all their diversity have developed, not merely to solve adaptive challenges, but also in response to the inchoate sense that we live before the face of God. Theologically, we could say that there is a seventh moral intuition, the pair that makes sense of the other six: answerability versus autonomy. This intuition assumes the biblical account in which humans have been entrusted with the "office" of a divine image bearer. In this office, we are responsible for how we meet God's call to make something of the world.

Let us explore this theme of answerability.[22] The image of God has often been understood in terms of resemblance (our faculties) or representation (our function). Both aspects, however, are rooted in a dialogical relationship between God and humanity. There is call and response; God addresses humanity and expects an answer. As Kevin Vanhoozer notes, "Surely it is significant that the only created species with which God entered into conversation was the human. To be sure, the Genesis account repeats 'God said' several times, but only in [Gen.] 1:28 do we read 'to them.' This is a defining moment in the history of the *imago Dei*. What makes men and women 'like God' has to do with their *being spoken to* and their capacity to *speak back*. Individuality is more a matter of *answerability* ('Here am I') than of assertability ('I think, therefore I am')."[23] To be made in God's image means to be a creature capable of answering God's call; indeed, it means to compose a life in response to God's initiating action. We are gifted with creative agency, the ability to take up the pen and write some lines of our own story. Unlike God, who authors *ex nihilo*, we work within the constraints of creatureliness and culture, within the limitations of bodies, communities, times, and places. We are answerable to the communities in which we find ourselves, and so it should not surprise us that our moral intuitions are deeply shaped by those relationships. But the deepest moral truth about us, whether as individuals or as cultures, is that we are answerable to God. This gives every human culture and every human person inherent dignity, even as it also provides inescapable duties.

Even in a fallen world, God continues to call out ("Where are you?" Gen. 3:9) and to engage humanity in covenantal address. Distanced from the divine voice, it is natural that we would seek legitimacy from a jury of our peers, who can confer on us a sense of righteousness. Indeed, our status as answerable agents means that we cannot escape the hunger for justification. The great temptation, represented in the words of the serpent, is to fall for the illusion of autonomy: "You will be like God, knowing good and evil" (Gen. 3:5). But autonomy is a lie. To declare freedom from our vocation as image bearers is merely to sell ourselves to idols. This truth is borne out, not just in the myriad addictions that modern culture cultivates—food, drink, sex, screens, and work—but also in our seculosity, our desire to satisfy the felt scrutiny of others to find the belonging, significance, and power we crave. The heart of human rebellion, Scripture shows us, is the hunger for autonomy, the desire to be emancipated from our office as divine image bearers, playing God in the process.[24]

Self-justification is an attempt at autonomy, an attempt to be the one who renders the final verdict on our life's work or cultural achievements.

But while self-examination can be salutary, we are in no position to make such decisive judgments. Here is Vanhoozer again:

> Teachers evaluate our academic work, friends our sociability, co-workers our competence, and so forth. Who is in a position to define me, to summarize my life and to evaluate me as a particular sort of person: selfish, selfless, proud, humble? Only one who can see my life as a whole—in a word, an author. Who is in a position to judge how well I have responded to my fundamental vocation of being answerable? Only the one to whom I am ultimately answerable for what I have authored: the Author. To be answerable to others and above all to God is our human vocation.[25]

All humans, Paul reminds us, have a law "written on their hearts," a law that internally condemns and approves of our behavior (Rom. 2:15). Our sense of righteousness can still be mediated culturally, but the transcendent source gives metaphysical weight to our moral judgments while also calling them into question. The conviction that our moral intuitions are underwritten by the divine can be dangerous, tempting us to claim canonical priority for cultural preferences. But it also gives a sense of gravity, the apprehension that we are answerable to a higher Power, one not of our making, before whose final judgment we will stand or fall.

Answerability has two foundational implications for our pursuit of righteousness. First, answerability relativizes the judgments of any given culture (its sense of righteousness) to the judgments of the Lord, which are "true and righteous altogether" (Ps. 19:9 KJV). Scripture provides us with a transformative element that calls cultural practices, movements, and institutions into question. Christian ethical reflection requires us to resolve the tension between our fidelity to Christ and all other cultural ties (to family, community, political party, country, etc.).[26] Our desire to belong to a community (by satisfying its requirements) need not always compete with our sacred office. But local allegiances must also not be allowed to trump our more fundamental allegiance to God. When judged by the story of Scripture, every culture has misdirected cultural norms, misguided mores, and unjust laws. In such cases, allegiance to God may call us to countercultural living, subversive discipleship, and civil disobedience. As Peter and the apostles told the Sanhedrin, "We must obey God rather than human beings" (Acts 5:29).

Answerability also means that while moral judgments are necessary, they are also provisional. Remembering this should keep us from the hubris of assuming that we always have the moral high ground. I have always found comments by Dr. King, offered in the heart of the struggle for civil rights, deeply convicting:

> A big danger for us is to follow the people we are opposing. . . . We must not end up with stereotypes of those we oppose, even as they slip all of us into their stereotypes. . . . Let us not try to put ourselves into one all-inclusive category—the virtuous ones against the evil ones, or the decent ones against the malicious, prejudiced ones, or the well-educated against the ignorant. You can see that I can go on and on—and there is the danger; the "us" or "them" mentality takes hold and we do, actually, begin to run the risk of joining ranks with the very people we are opposing.[27]

This is one reason why the iconoclasm of complication is usually preferable to the iconoclasm of cancellation (discussed in the previous chapter): cancellation includes the temptation to deify ourselves after we have slain the old gods. The moment that we begin to congratulate ourselves, as if justice and goodness were *our* invention rather than God's gift, we move from answerability to autonomy. Scripture gives us no room for self-righteousness, no ground for the smug satisfaction of placing ourselves above and apart, or for excluding our enemy, as Miroslav Volf puts it, "from the community of humans" while excluding ourselves "from the community of sinners."[28]

The apostle Paul wrote to the Corinthians, "I care very little if I am judged by you or by any human court; indeed, I do not even judge myself. My conscience is clear, but that does not make me innocent. It is the Lord who judges me" (1 Cor. 4:3–4). Our answerability to God does not clear us of accountability to others, but it does relativize all human judgments. The Christian story tells us that there is a judge in heaven, the only one who can be trusted to render a final ruling. This give us hope, beyond all imagining, that everything wrong will in some fundamental way be made right. God, the source of all justice, will judge all the nations of the world (Ps. 98:9; Matt. 25:31–46). As individuals and as cultures, we are answerable; and indeed, a verdict is coming. God "will repay each person according to what they have done" (Rom. 2:6). Though they are often uttered in bad faith, no words could be truer, more terrifying, and more transformative than these: "Only God can judge me."

Only by grace will any withstand the test. For in our hunger for justification, the gospel offers solid food: "Since we have been justified through faith, we have peace with God through our Lord Jesus Christ, through whom we have gained access by faith into this grace in which we now stand" (Rom. 5:1–2). Righteousness is found in being rightly related to Christ, the true and prototypical image of God (Col. 1:18). Justification means being accepted and acceptable before God, included and incorporated in Christ and in his people. Thus, whenever we speak about being or becoming better humans, Christians start and stay with the Spirit-filled humanity of Jesus Christ. Goodness is always a gift before it is a goal; it is never an autonomous human achievement. The source of virtue, for Christians, is faith: trust in and allegiance to Jesus Christ as Lord.[29]

It is precisely because we live for the applause of heaven that we can embrace the demands of discipleship, which call us to a higher standard than the mores of local culture and community. These demands include a call to seek public justice, but also to practice obscurity and secrecy. "Be careful not to practice your righteousness in front of others to be seen by them," Jesus tells us. "If you do, you will have no reward from your Father in heaven" (Matt. 6:1). To be—rather than to appear—seems a fitting outcome of answerable Christian discipleship: that any moral claims we make would first make their claim on us. This brings me to a second theological thread.

Theological Thread 2: Stewardship and Servanthood

We return finally to the subject of power, but to power as the original gift of creative love rather than the fallen reality of coercive domination.[30] Redeeming power requires more than the rejection of its toxic exercise. It also requires a renewed sense of our vocation as image bearers who use our creative agency for the flourishing of creation. Here we can also note the trinitarian shape of our endeavors. Flourishing requires accountability to the Creator and a concern for the good of our fellow creatures. Flourishing must be forged through self-sacrificial love, following the pattern of the Crucified King. And flourishing must be measured by the signs of the Spirit, especially righteousness, peace, and joy. Let us take these one at a time.

First, whatever power we have, it is the power of stewards—entrusted with precious things—and "what is sought in stewards is that one be found faithful" (1 Cor. 4:2 NET). In his excellent book *We Answer to Another*, David Koyzis recounts the Milgram experiments, in which participants were tested to see how far they would follow directives to administer electrical shocks to human subjects. As it turns out, participants were willing to go quite far in inflicting pain if they could say they were "just following orders." There were at least two participants, however, who dropped out earlier than the rest, and both attributed this refusal to religious convictions. Koyzis writes that these two were not simply escaping authority to claim their own autonomy but rather were submitting to another, higher authority, one to whom they felt accountable.[31] To recognize our ultimate accountability to God means that we must always seek to place ourselves in accountability to responsible others. These authorities themselves must remain accountable, sensitive to the limitations of their office, transparent to correction.

For it is certainly the case—as we will see in the next chapter—that religious justification could be leveraged in service of coercive power rather than against it. (The rally cry of the Crusades was "God wills it!") And it is for this reason that power, in the hands of Christian disciples, must take on a cruciform shape. There is a profound difference between the sort of power promised by political candidates and the sort promised by Jesus himself in the book of Acts.[32] "But you will receive power when the Holy Spirit comes on you," Jesus told his disciples. "And you will be my witnesses in Jerusalem, and in all Judea and Samaria, and to the ends of the earth" (Acts 1:8). The power that is given to the church is the power to be witnesses. We rightly refer to the church as "the body of Christ," those who seek to embody Christ's kingdom to the world. But let us remember the character of the kingdom: "You know that the rulers of the Gentiles lord it over them, and their high officials exercise authority over them. Not so with you. Instead, whoever wants to become great among you must be your servant, and whoever wants to be first must be your slave—just as the Son of Man did not come to be served, but to serve, and to give his life as a ransom for many" (Matt. 20:25–28). Christ's power is not coercive. It is not lording power over others but rather taking up the identity of a servant: "I am among you as one who serves" (Luke 22:27). The power of a servant is the power to move to the margins, to seek to make others successful, to consider others more significant than yourself. Only when the church exercises its power in this way does it faithfully continue the ministry of Christ. As J. H. Bavinck writes, to read the gospel with full attention of heart is to "make the discovery that Jesus is different, that His power is different from all other types of power in the world, because the power of Jesus is identical with His self-sacrificing love."[33]

Consider J. R. R. Tolkien's answer to Glaucon's challenge, in his *Lord of the Rings* trilogy. In the epic, the Ruling Ring represents the desire for autonomy, to be limitless (undying) and unaccountable (invisible), exercising mastery over the wills of others. By contrast, to refuse the ring is to embrace limits, to remain accountable, and to seek to live at peace with others. It is the refusal to play God. Once the ring is found, the heroes decide not to use it (even for good!) but to destroy it.[34] While desire for the ring bewitches most in Middle-earth, the powerful wizard Gandalf refuses the temptation. When pressed by another character (Denethor, the high steward of Gondor) to justify his choices, Gandalf replies, "The rule of no realm is mine, neither of Gondor nor any other, great or small. But all worthy things that are in peril as the world now stands, those are my care. And for my part, I shall not wholly fail of my task, though Gondor should perish, if anything passes through this night that can still grow fair or bear fruit and flower again in days to come. For I also am a steward. Did you not know?"[35] "I also am a steward." In other words, "I don't answer to you, but I do answer to someone." Heroic virtue in Gandalf's case cannot be explained as a matter of repu- tation management. Rather, it is a recognition of his answerability as a steward who seeks to make space where things can "grow fair or bear fruit and flower again in days to come." Such stewardship means a dif- ferent understanding of power, the power of a servant and steward, not a lord and master.

This brings us finally to norms for Christian flourishing. What sort of community does accountable, self-sacrificing love create? We can follow Volf, together with his coauthor Ryan McAnnally-Linz, who translates the ethical categories discussed earlier in the chapter as "leading life well," "life going well," and "life feeling good." Each of these emphases has robust representation throughout ethical theory, and for good reason. To use biblical language, if "leading life well" is an expression of *righteousness*, then, "life going well" is an expression of *peace*, the biblical concept of shalom. Finally, though, "life feeling good" cannot stand on its own as the criterion for flourishing; when righteousness and peace are present, there will also be *joy*, which "sums up what life in the kingdom feels like."[36] These three elements are marks of the kingdom ruled by Christ: "righteousness, peace and joy in the Holy Spirit" (Rom. 14:17). When it comes to discerning these marks, we have reasons for both confidence and caution. As Wolterstorff reminds us,

> The solution is not to refrain from identifying the signs of Christ's redemptive rule but to resist the arrogance of supposing that our identifications are indubitably correct and complete. . . . Likewise we resist the arrogance of supposing that the signs of Christ's redemptive action coincide with the goals of our successful endeavors. . . . Christian hope for the righting of injustice is both confident as to its ground in Christ and humble as to its ability to discern the ways in which our endeavors contribute to the coming of Christ's rule of justice.[37]

Acknowledging these limitations, we nevertheless can name these as our ethical norms. Righteousness, peace, and joy—as defined by the Scriptures and discerned in Christian community—mark the moral order that we are called to steward and serve in every culture where we have been placed.

Distinctive Practice: Organic Servanthood

This brings us to the distinctive practice of the ethical dimension, which I will call "organic servanthood." I am using this word "organic" after the manner of Antonio Gramsci, who imagined a revolution led by "organic intellectuals," not from the safety of the academic balcony but from a more vulnerable place on the street. An organic intellectual seeks to be vitally connected, living among the people she seeks to serve.[38] Few are called to be public intellectuals of this sort. But every one of us is called to be an organic servant, a steward of creation and of whatever power we possess. Here power is the creative ability to take whatever situation we are given and to seek to make it better. Every Christian is called to be a servant, seeking the welfare of the communities to whom we are integrally connected, and a steward who is ultimately answerable to the Lord.

The word "organic" also evokes a stunning image of new creation found in the prophecies of Micah (see also 1 Kings 4:25 and Zech. 3:10). The prophet imagines the nations streaming toward the holy mountain to be taught by Yahweh, who will judge between the peoples and settle disputes between nations. The result of Yahweh's justice is that "everyone will sit under their own vine and under their own fig tree, and no one will make them afraid" (Mic. 4:4).

The vision of moral order that we find in prophets like Micah is a vision of safety and security, health and harmony with creation, flourishing and freedom from fear. We wait for God's dramatic intervention to fully realize this end. But our anticipation of that intervention does not prevent us from laboring to make "imperfect models of the good world that is to come."[39] It does not prevent us from laboring to make room for all members of our community to have their own space for creative love, their own garden to tend. It does not prevent us from resisting whatever real evils fill the human family with fear.

Whenever I take my students through this text, I remind them that there is nothing wrong with hoping to flourish, wanting to sit under your own vine and fig tree without fear. But this vision compels us to ask what keeps our neighbors from being able to do so as well, to inquire about what sorts of things are making them afraid, and then seeking to do something about it. For it is because we "walk in the name of the LORD our God for ever and ever" (Mic. 4:5) that we seek to steward and to serve this vision of the end in our local communities and in the wider culture.

We walk humbly (Mic. 6:8), in the name of our God, the One who has joined us at our table, sharing our food, and suffering our violence. His continuing presence interrogates our practices. For though Jesus is not averse to flipping the tables (John 2:13–17), his more common practice is to sit at them, asking penetrating questions. When Jesus sits at the table, he draws our attention to who is sitting in the place of honor and who has been left out. He exposes our attempts to be in the center and to avoid the voices of those on the margins (Luke 14:8–14). And he reminds us that God's kingdom runs in the opposite direction of every human culture on earth: *toward* the outsiders.

Our cultural stories provide moral matrices, limits within which we seek to flourish. This ethical dimension offers competing visions of the good life, and of what it means to belong. But if we can only find righteousness in fellowship with God, then the religious dimension of culture cannot be reduced to its moral sensibilities. It is rather a layer all its own, and to that dimension we now turn.

QUESTIONS FOR
REFLECTION AND DISCUSSION

1. The chapter opened with a story about being stopped by a security guard. What are some other common situations that produce wildly different moral intuitions? What is a situation that triggered one of your moral intuitions (making you say, "This is not right!")?

2. What are some of the most common moral frameworks you've encountered? How do various groups answer questions about what is right and wrong? How might Moral Foundations Theory illuminate some of our moral disagreements?

3. What do you make of the argument from Glaucon and Jonathan Haidt that people are content with having a reputation for righteousness rather than with righteousness itself? What do we lose if we reduce moral behavior to the desire to signal that we belong to a group?

4. What is your understanding of what it means to be answerable to God? What implications does that have on the way that you pursue "righteousness"?

5. What could the practice of organic servanthood look like in the various communities to which you belong? What could it mean to serve and steward the vision of the prophet Micah in which "everyone will sit under their own vine and under their own fig tree, and no one will make them afraid" (4:4)?

6. How do we make space for and move toward outsiders in everyday life, as well as in cultural spaces and institutions? What are the difficulties that attend such a move?

THE RELIGIOUS DIMENSION

Culture as Sacred Experience

One of my favorite actors is the legendary comedian Bill Murray. I recently stumbled across an interview in which Murray was asked to name a piece of art that had made a difference in his life. He shared a story of surprising vulnerability, recounting a time early in his career when he was living in Chicago and a failed audition took him to a dark place. He considered throwing himself into Lake Michigan, and as he walked in that direction, he passed Chicago's Art Institute and went in. There he encountered a painting, *The Song of the Lark*, which depicts a woman working in a field as the sun rises behind her. Here is how Murray told it: "I saw it that day, and I said, there's a girl who doesn't have a whole lot of prospects. But the sun's coming up anyway. And she's got another chance at it. I think that gave me some sort of feeling that I too am a person and get another chance every day the sun comes up."[1] Whatever the original artist may have intended, there was something *human* represented in the painting, something that connected across time, space, class, and culture. The connection was so profoundly felt that it may have saved Murray's life.

In a class I teach on Christianity and pop culture, I ask students something similar to the question from the interview: tell me about a piece of popular culture that has really mattered to you. The students must be drawn out because their comfort zones tend to be in two modes: amusement or critique. On the one hand, they can talk freely about their favorite movies, songs, and shows; they can laugh as they quote an episode or tell me every word of an album. Alternatively, they can tell me everything wrong with their favorites from a Christian point of view. (They think this is what I want to hear.) But when pressed to consider *why* particular pieces mean so much to them, they retreat as if they are being asked to expose some secret. Some are hesitant: "I don't know; I just like it." Others are resistant: "I don't want to overanalyze it; that would ruin the enjoyment." But occasionally the responses are quite moving. Students share how a piece of pop culture gave them a way to name their experience, changed their mind about something important, helped them cope with discouragement, or connected them to loved ones. As more students share, a sense of collective recognition washes over the room. It is as if we are all surprised to find that something so apparently trivial could move us so deeply.

The pieces of pop culture that affect my students, like the painting that saved Murray, are complex phenomena, open to analysis from multiple angles. *The Song of the Lark* is part of a series that depicts nineteenth-century peasants working in fields; as such, it is ripe for interpretation through lenses of power and class. Similarly, pop culture artifacts are commodities in an "attention economy" that seeks to fill all our free time and space. Discerning how these artifacts constrain and manufacture human desire has an important place, as we have seen. Yet an exclusive focus on manipulation and malformation misses the *human* element, without which we would feel no resonance.

In other words, culture cannot be reduced to coercion. Although all cultural actions, artifacts, and institutions are situated by power dynamics, none of these things will be fully seen through the critical lens. This is even true when it comes to works that contain critiques of power, like Tolkien's *Lord of the Rings* trilogy. Given Tolkien's experiences in the Great War, it is not difficult to see how "One Ring to rule them all" serves as a commentary on the misuse of power in general and on the Great War in particular.[2] Yet Tolkien himself resisted the interpretation. Instead, he wrote, "The tale is not really about Power and Dominion: that only sets the wheels going; it is about Death and the desire for deathlessness. Which is hardly more than to say it is a tale written by a Man!"[3] Tolkien suggests that a fundamental element of human storytelling is wrestling with (and perhaps resisting) the facts of our finitude. We create culture in recognition and defiance of the reality of death. If the ethical dimension of culture is where we seek moral limits within which we can flourish, then a different dimension exists in which we wrestle with and seek to transcend the limits of creaturely life. I will call this the religious dimension of culture.

This may seem counterintuitive, since culture often seems to distract us from thinking about our limits and from embracing the finality of death. It is for this reason that culture and religion are so often set in antithesis. Culture is imagined to be superficial, pulling us away from the depths of contemplation, from remembering that we will die (memento mori). Like a flashing screen in a restaurant, the amusements of mass culture keep us overstimulated, unable to focus on the matter at hand. I don't want to overstate this point because, at times, diversion is precisely what we need. People who have experienced trauma, for example, will speak of distraction as a necessary tonic, a welcome relief. But distraction cannot be a long-term strategy or organizing pattern for life. Our engagement with culture must shift from distraction and consumption to creativity and contemplation, becoming a means to more grounded, meaningful lives.

A more sophisticated account of the relationship between culture making and death is found in Ernest Becker's acclaimed book *The Denial of Death*. Becker argues that the major engine of human culture is the unconscious desire to avoid mortality. Thus, we don't merely distract ourselves with cultural fare; we also seek deathlessness in some larger project that will outlive us: a family, a legacy, a nation, an empire. The result is that every culture is covertly religious, filled with "immortality projects," which means that culture wars are inevitably "holy wars," my immortality project against yours.[4] Here coercive power rears its head once again. In this case, religion acts as an *intensifier*, supercharging our cultural pursuits, which we trust will save us from being forgotten forever.

The connection between culture, community, and mortality is also explored memorably in Swedish filmmaker Ingmar Bergman's 1957 film *The Seventh Seal*. In the film, a knight named Antonius Block plays chess with Death and debates his adversary throughout the film about the meaning of life:

> Block: I want knowledge! Not faith, not assumptions, but knowledge. I want God to stretch out His hand, uncover His face, and speak to me.
>
> Death: But He remains silent.
>
> Block: I call out to Him in the darkness. But it's as if no one was there.
>
> Death: Perhaps there isn't anyone.
>
> Block: Then life is a preposterous horror. No man can live faced with Death, knowing everything's nothingness.
>
> Death: Most people think neither of death nor nothingness.
>
> Block: But one day you stand at the edge of life and face darkness.[5]

Block, who feels that his crusader's life has been misguided and meaningless, makes it his aim to accomplish "one meaningful deed" before he dies. This leads him to form a company of travelers, and together they journey through a plague-ridden land, fleeing from (but also toward) Death, who is never far away.

Becker and Bergman have both placed their finger on something significant about culture. We resonate with particular cultural artifacts and gravitate toward particular communities because they help us to cope and connect amid the anxieties of our time. They offer us a way to draw together with others, mining the depths of shared human experience, dealing with existential despair and the specter of our death. Community is formed around these common human experiences, in which we identify a layer of life that is sacred. The discipline of religious studies, itself composed of various sociological, psychological, and phenomenological approaches, seeks to understand this sacred dimension. In this chapter I will examine its contribution to our understanding of culture, even amid the need for a more explicitly theological approach. This will lead me to pull on two theological threads: (1) connection and community and (2) religion and revelation. The distinctive practice that will emerge is directional discernment, an exploration of what a person or culture is doing with God.

What Qualifies as Religious? In Search of Solidarity

Religion is notoriously difficult to define. Common accounts of religion revolve around belief in the supernatural, experiences of transcendence, or institutional affiliation. But the idea of religion "as a great objective something" is itself a modern development; outside the Western world, the idea of separating religion and culture as distinct entities seems strange. In this perspective, all of life has religious significance.[6] Indeed, in my class on popular culture, students smile when they realize just how often they use the adverb "religiously" (e.g., "I watch that show religiously"). Religiosity is connected to regularity, and yet it is not enough to say, "I watch it regularly." To say we watch a show religiously, or "work out religiously," or "read the news religiously" signals an additional layer of *concern* (it is important to me) and *consistency* (it orders and integrates my everyday life). There is a field of study called "implicit religion" that investigates these ordinary occurrences of religiosity: the more extensive and integrative something is, the more religious it is deemed to be.[7] For although not all humans are adherents of a particular *religion*, we all live *religiously*.

Consider the rise of those who identify as "spiritual but not religious." This may describe those who are disillusioned with traditional religion yet still hunger for "something more." Or perhaps in a world where we are used to having options, it represents the desire for a more customized spirituality.[8] The problem with this sort of "do-it-yourself" spirituality, however, is that it places an incredible burden on the individual to forge the depth of meaning once freely given in historic traditions. Personalized spirituality feels thin; something more robust is required. This has led some, like psychologist Jason Smith, to opt for the strange phrase "religious but not religious." It means saying no to being religious in the sense of affirming dogmatic constructions about the way the world works. But it means saying yes to being religious in the sense of participating in the symbolic depths of existence, depths that are attested by religions and craved by the human psyche.[9] In this sense, at least, we are inescapably religious, hungering for something that will help us—in the face of our limits—to learn what it means to live.

Like the knight in Bergman's film, this usually leads us to gather with some sort of fellowship: a church or something like it. A pair of Harvard seminarians compiled a report called *How We Gather*, which considers the ways that millennials were congregating outside traditional religious institutions. They studied fitness communities like SoulCycle alongside community-building organizations like the Dinner Party (which organizes meals around conversations about loss) and Camp Grounded ("summer camp for adults"). They found that these organizations fulfilled a religious function in the lives of the participants, following six primary themes:

1. Community: valuing and fostering deep relationships that center on service to others
2. Personal transformation: making a conscious and dedicated effort to develop one's own body, mind, and spirit
3. Social transformation: pursuing justice and beauty in the world through the creation of networks for good
4. Purpose finding: clarifying, articulating, and acting on one's personal mission in life
5. Creativity: allowing time and space to activate the imagination and engage in play
6. Accountability: holding oneself and others responsible for working toward defined goals

For the authors of the study, the emergence of these new gatherings is a sign of spiritual health and hope, even against the backdrop of diminishing religious affiliation.[10]

Similarly, Tara Isabella Burton's book *Strange Rites* explores the contours of what she calls "new religions for a godless world." These "intuitional religions" seek to curate communal experiences marked by personal feeling and authenticity. Burton finds signs of remixed religion in all sorts of cultural trends:

If you've ever been to a yoga studio or CrossFit class, ever practiced "self-care" with a ten-step Korean beauty routine or a Gwyneth Paltrow–sanctioned juice cleanse, . . . ever compared your spiritual outlook to a Dungeons and Dragons classification ("lawful good, chaotic evil") or your personal temperament to that of a Hogwarts house, ever channeled your sense of cosmic purpose into social justice activism, ever tried to "bio-hack" yourself or used a meditation app like Headspace, ever negotiated "personal relationship rules"—be they kink or ethical nonmonogamy—with a partner, ever cleansed a house with sage, or ever been wary of a person's "toxic energy," you've participated in some of these trends.[11]

Burton argues that just as it is impossible to understand the Protestant Reformation apart from the technology of the printing press, it is impossible to understand the emergence of these religious forms apart from the power of the internet, which excels at connecting kindred spirits across distance. The appeal of these new communities of belonging lies in how they scratch a religious itch. For although many of these trends are novel and faddish, they cast a religious spell because they tap into something old and enduring, the traditional pillars of religion: *meaning, purpose, community,* and *ritual.* But although Burton finds these communities fascinating, she also finds them wanting, poor substitutes for more "well-developed ethical, moral, and metaphysical systems." And since they are often driven by corporate interests seeking to commodify the experience of connection, the best they can offer is "psychic methadone . . . a brief and illusory hit of moral belonging."[12]

In describing religious belonging as "psychic methadone," Burton is not just speaking metaphorically. Jonathan Haidt, too, compares this "hit of belonging" to the flipping of a "hive switch," where an experience causes us to feel that we are connected to something larger than ourselves. When the switch is flipped, we are more likely to sacrifice our self-interest, behave "groupishly," and act on behalf of our community. Haidt shows how experiences as diverse as awe in nature, participation in team-based competition, and the use of psychedelic drugs have all been shown to trip the hive switch, making us feel the euphoria of being part of a larger whole.[13] The religious impulse, with its hunger to connect to something larger and lasting, seems to be hardwired into us.

Both Burton and Haidt are working from an influential account of religion framed by the father of sociology, Émile Durkheim. For Durkheim, religion is about *belonging* before it is about *believing,* and if this the case, we should not be surprised by the strange things that groups of people are able to believe. What binds groups together, he believed, is not necessarily truth but the solidarity that is found in a shared apprehension of reality. It is when we feel connected to others, and to something bigger than ourselves, that we enter the realm of the sacred. Durkheim called the intensely felt power of communal experience "collective efferves-cence," which describes the "sort of electricity" that is "generated from closeness," launching us "to an extraordinary height of exaltation."[14] Imagine the energy shared among seventy thousand people who have just witnessed a game-winning score, which leads fans (a word that is short for "fanatic," of course) not just to scream and shout but also to embrace total strangers in celebration. Or imagine the ecstasy of attend-ing a concert and joining an unnumbered multitude in singing a common song. "Ecstasy" is the right word; it conveys the sense of being pulled outside of yourself and into a sacred solidarity that extends beyond the ordinary bonds of kinship.

But religion offers something even more potent than solidarity when it comes to culture. It offers *legitimation*. Religion authorizes a culture's practices, pursuits, and institutions by nesting them in a sacred order, or to use the famous phrase from sociologist Peter Berger, in a "sacred canopy." Berger describes the making of a cultural world as a cycle of externalization (we imagine our place in the world), objectivation (we perceive that world as objectively real), and internalization (we reapply objectivated reality to ourselves). This process, when blessed by religious authorities, offers "structure legitimation"; it grants legitimacy to the social order, allowing us to live in an ordered, meaningful world.[15]

Religious justification persists, even in disenchanted societies. We consistently feel the need to establish a priestly class, a group of people who are somehow more attuned to reality and who can let us know the way forward.[16] We may give the priestly mantle to scientists and ask them to save us from aging and disease. Or we give it to pundits who claim to cut through the spin and tell us what is really going on. Or perhaps we give the priestly mantle to our celebrities, the bold and beautiful ones who embody our hopes and dreams of what the good life could be. But our priests, whoever they are, reassure us that we are moving in the right direction, that our vision of the world is basically true, and that every-thing will be fine if we do our part.

The problem with this, of course, is that history attests to the great evils that religious authorities (of both theistic and secular varieties) have been willing to legitimize. Slovenian philosopher Slavoj Žižek puts this sharply, arguing that since killing another human being is deeply traumatic, we can only be convinced to do it in service of a sacred cause, "something that makes petty individual concerns about killing seem trivial." He turns Dostoevsky's dictum on its head: "If there is a God, then anything is permitted."[17] Žižek has in mind not just religious crusaders who say "God wills it!" but also atheistic regimes that set themselves up in God's place. His point is that ideology always seeks some sort of religious blessing for violence so that we can defer responsibility to some absolute order and say, "This is the way it must be." The religious dimension not only intensifies culture but sanctifies its pathologies so that we are willing to do more than die for our group. We will also dehumanize, torture, and kill.

Let us take a moment to summarize this first section. Identifying the religious dimension of life has to do with noticing what humans regard as sacred, especially as they seek to cope with the complexities of life and the certainty of death. Not everything is religious, but anything can be invested with religious significance. Doing so creates a sacred solidarity that unites communities and cultures. When the things we treat religiously are trivial, they may offer a "hit of belonging," but they lack the expansiveness to organize our lives. Communities of belonging centered on these things are too shallow to offer us solid anchors for meaning. At worst they become addictions, idols that eat us alive if we look to them to save us.[18] But when the things we treat religiously are nontrivial, capable of organizing not just an individual life but the life of a culture, they rise to the level of a religious ideology. Here we meet more dangerous idols, like racism and nationalism, which are not content with their worshipers' ruin but also insist on the diminishment, degradation, and destruction of our neighbors.

Religion binds, but religion also blinds, which means that the religious dimension of culture needs considerable resources for self-criticism.[19] The question is not whether religious sensibilities will persist, in trivial or nontrivial forms. The question is whether the religious frameworks we adopt will be robust enough to organize an ethical life and to resist our darkest demons. Thus, there are two problems that we need to unravel. First, the function of religion has been described in purely horizontal terms, concerned with binding groups together in a shared reality and common pursuit. Does that leave any space for a real connection with ultimate reality, for communion with God? How can we know that what

we consider sacred is more than just another work of cultural imagination, an "immortality project" to distract us from the despair of death?

The second problem is that the religious impulse intensifies the bonds
of culture by connecting our cultural stories to a cosmic narrative of legitimation. But this is quite dangerous because it may lead us to suspend
ordinary ethical behavior for the sake of what God (or the ideology we
put in God's place) tells us to do. We need to ask if our religious systems
possess sufficient resources to escape the tendency to use religion as a
prop.

To deal with these questions, I will explore two theological threads.
The first thread will examine the link between the horizontal and ver-
tical dimension of religious life; the second thread will maintain that
revelation offers us a defense against the dangers of religion. For if it is
God's gracious involvement with humanity that triggers the desire for
sacred solidarity, then the religious impulse can only find its fulfillment
in God's gift, which possesses us without becoming our possession.

Theological Thread 1: Connection and Community

The sociological vision of religion (in which religion is mostly about
belonging) is preferable to accounts of religion that focus mainly on
the rationality of belief (like the "new atheists"). But the sociological
account is also incomplete because its horizon is limited to the human.
Insofar as it is content to describe the features of human religiosity, it
does not seek to make any claims as to whether people are in touch with
anything real. It studies religious belonging without the need for God to
be a transforming presence, even if it is open to that possibility.

Theologians of the nineteenth and twentieth centuries made valiant
efforts to reweave the severed connection between religious impulse and
metaphysical reality. Friedrich Schleiermacher (1768–1834) encouraged
"cultured despisers of religion" to start with religious feeling, the sort
that is evoked in nature or in the enjoyment of great music. If these
cultured despisers would look into the depths of their humanity, Schleiermacher believed, they would find a sense of absolute dependence,
which would imply Something or Someone on which they must depend.[20]

Rudolf Otto (1869–1937) shared this focus on experience, but he was concerned that Schleiermacher had only described human *self*-consciousness.

By contrast, Otto wanted to emphasize human encounters with holiness, which he called the "numinous." The numinous is felt as a fearful and fascinating mystery (*mysterium tremendum et fascinans*) that must be experienced to be understood.[21] It is the experience of Jacob at Bethel: "Surely the LORD is in this place, and I was not aware of it" (Gen. 28:16). Otto notes that when we encounter the numinous, we feel a spontaneous movement toward "self-disvaluation": "Woe to me! . . . I am ruined!" (Isa. 6:5); "Depart from me, for I am a sinful man" (Luke 5:8 ESV). We immediately recognize, Otto says, that something is out there, something that exceeds us in kind, not just degree. It might destroy us if we dare approach it. And yet, we do not dare not to dare.

Some of the most poignant encounters with the numinous are found in children's stories, such as Kenneth Grahame's *The Wind in the Willows*. In Grahame's story, friends Rat and Mole find themselves unexpectedly in a holy place:

> "This is the place of my song-dream, the place the music played to me," whispered the Rat, as if in a trance. "Here, in this holy place, here if anywhere, surely we shall find Him!"
>
> Then suddenly the Mole felt a great Awe fall upon him, an awe that turned his muscles to water, bowed his head, and rooted his feet to the ground. It was no panic terror—indeed he felt wonderfully at peace and happy—but it was an awe that smote and held him and, without seeing, he knew it could only mean that some august Presence was very, very near. With difficulty he turned to look for his friend and saw him at his side cowed, stricken, and trembling violently. . . .
>
> "Rat!" he found breath to whisper, shaking. "Are you afraid?"
>
> "Afraid?" murmured the Rat, his eyes shining with unutterable love. "Afraid! Of Him? O, never, never! And yet—and yet—O, Mole, I am afraid!"[22]

The sense that we are profane in the presence of holiness leads to covering, the need for shelter, the felt necessity of atonement. Yet because the numinous also enchants and attracts us, we long "to transcend this sundering unworthiness."[23] For Otto, it is the experience of holiness that triggers humanity's religious impulse.

Yet many will say that they have had no such experience, or that it belongs to a lost, enchanted world, which is why we can only now find such reports in fairy tales. This led other theologians, like Paul Tillich (1886–1965), to follow Schleiermacher's strategy of unearthing religious reality from the depths of the human soul. Defining religion as a sense of "ultimate concern," Tillich writes, "Religion opens up the depth of man's spiritual life which is usually covered by the dust of our daily life and the noise of our secular work. It gives us the experience of the Holy, of something which is untouchable, awe-inspiring, an ultimate meaning, the source of ultimate courage."[24] The experience of the Holy is found not above or outside us but beneath and within us, buried by the dust of daily life. It is the haunting question in the depth of our soul. Culture externalizes our religious depths, and we cannot understand a culture without discovering its greatest anxiety and its greatest hope. And the dominant anxiety in the modern world, Tillich believed, is the one that plagues Bergman's knight: meaninglessness in the face of our mortality.

David Tracy similarly seeks to correlate Christian tradition with common human experience.[25] The religious dimension, Tracy writes, responds to what he called "limit-experiences," experiences that disclose a fuller dimension to life: "sickness, guilt, anxiety, and the recognition of death as one's own destiny," but also "love, joy, the creative act, profound reassurance." All of these are "authentically self-transcending moments in our lives."[26]

Most of us know what Tracy is talking about: the birth of a child, the loss of a loved one, the accomplishment of a life goal, the experience of synchronicity with a team or troupe. These become defining experiences in our lives. I can easily recall an experience I had the summer after my freshman year of college when I had the opportunity to spend ten weeks in Siberia with a group of fellow students. At the beginning of the summer, our group undertook an expedition to a remote location that required us to hike and then row a massive-oared boat across a lake. Desiring to deliver Bibles to the remote location, we took the bare minimum of food for the trip, mostly crackers, instant oatmeal, candy bars, and a few cans of tuna fish. I remember what it was like eating the tuna fish (straight out of the can) and thinking, "This is the best meal I've ever had." It wasn't because of what it was; it was because of what it meant. What that tuna fish represented was not just a full stomach but a full soul, the feeling that I would rather be in that boat with those people than anywhere else in the world. In that moment, my life made sense and mattered in a way that I have felt only a few times since.

Limit-experiences take us to the heights and the depths of our humanity, and in that journey, we feel that there is truth. Indeed, the reason why some cultural artifacts stand the test of time, Tracy says, is because we recognize in them a disclosure of reality that surprises, challenges, and transforms us. These are classic works, "certain expressions of the human spirit [that] so disclose a compelling truth about our lives that we cannot deny them some kind of normative status." The authority of these cultural artifacts does not derive from validation by the powerful or by popular vote. Their authority is discerned by a spirit of recognition: "What we mean in naming certain texts, events, images, rituals, symbols and persons 'classics' is that here we recognize nothing less than the disclosure of a reality we cannot but name truth."[27] Classics move us because they speak to our limit-questions and limit-experiences. In them, "deep calls to deep" (Ps. 42:7). We are not drawn to classics simply because we feel connection but because we believe they are disclosing reality, telling us something that is *true*.

Tracy takes one further step, arguing that unlike cultural classics, which address particular areas of human life, *religious* classics address the whole of existence. They involve "a claim to truth as the event of a disclosure-concealment of the whole of reality *by the power of the whole*—as, in some sense, a radical and finally gracious mystery."[28] Note that on Tracy's account, while anything can become religious, not everything can become a religion, which must offer a comprehensive scope, a fruitful (though not necessarily final) vision of the way things really are. To understand the religious dimension of culture, it is not enough to show how religious belonging binds people together on a horizontal plane. We must also account for the "verticality" of religion, how it roots us *down* in deeper soil and how it raises us *up* toward a higher reality. To put it another way, common concerns bind us together precisely because they address our deepest questions, precisely because in them we hear a call to be caught up and transformed.

This "emotional-expressivist" account of religion, which seeks God in religious feeling, has been criticized for its tendency to focus on religious experience in general rather than on the particulars. It can sometimes sound as if the feeling of transcendence is all that matters, and any experience will do, so long as it makes us feel our finitude. As George Lindbeck has argued, *particular* religions produce *particular* experiences, and it is precisely the concrete practices and promises of faith that matter to the faithful.[29] There is a difference, however, between attempting to translate every religion into a universal religious experience and recognizing how creaturely finitude triggers a religious response in many concrete forms. Here we run into another version of the original problem: If religious visions vary so widely, then how can we discern truth between differing interpretations? And how do we know whether our "religious classics" are disclosing what *is* rather than projecting what we wish would be?

The critique of religion comes not just from outside the walls of the church but also from within. Consider the case of German theologian Dietrich Bonhoeffer (1906–1945), who watched with horror as the Christianity of his native country was used to prop up the Nazi regime. Rather than offering a substantive challenge to Hitler, nineteenth-century theology prepared the way, leaving Christians unable to distinguish between the reach of the Third Reich and the hand of God. After participating in a failed attempt to assassinate Hitler, Bonhoeffer was executed in a Nazi concentration camp, just days before Allied liberation.

Imprisoned at the end of his life, Bonhoeffer began to write about the possibility of a "religionless Christianity." The phrase is provocative and undeveloped, puzzling scholars as to its meaning. But it is at least clear that Bonhoeffer was criticizing the way that religion tends to employ God as a stopgap: God is brought in as the solution to our unanswered questions, the support for our unstable projects, the satisfaction of our unfulfilled aspirations. Even worse, God is brought in to bless our lust for worldly power. This allows us to set the terms for God's involvement, as if the heart of God's work were to resolve human problems. How could this God be anything more than a human projection? Rather than beginning with ourselves, Bonhoeffer wrote, we must begin with what God is doing, allowing God to occupy the space at the very center of life: "God is no stopgap; he must be recognized as the center of life, not when we are at the end of our resources; it is his will to be recognized in life, and not only when death comes; in health and vigor, and not only in suffering; in our activities, and not only in sin. The ground for this lies in the revelation of God in Jesus Christ. He is the center of life, and he certainly didn't 'come' to answer our unsolved problems."[30] In other words, there is a difference between employing a God-concept at the edges of our experience—as a way to solve the problem of sin, cope with suffering, or escape death—and hearing God's call to radical discipleship in every part of life, regardless of whether this solves our problems. Such a transformation can never happen through human legitimation; it can only happen through divine revelation, through God telling us something we do not already know and that we could never tell ourselves. This brings us to my second thread.

Theological Thread 2: Religion and Revelation

American evangelicals are fond of saying that Christianity is "not a religion but a relationship." This truism is a sensibility that is not limited to Christianity. South African Muslim Farid Esack, for example, writes of the way that his relationship with Allah funds his work as an activist. He calls his fellow Muslims to join him on a path "between the . . . fuzzy love of God" and "the relentless coldness of a distant Transcendent Being." For Esack, being radical about Islam means a path "committed to social justice, to individual liberty and the quest for the Transcendent."[31] Christians need to be exposed to testimonies like this, which complicate our perceptions of non-Christian religions in general and of Islam in particular. Esack's profession of faith raises a theological question: Is there any way that Christians can say that his devotional activism is the fruit of a life-giving connection to the God revealed in Jesus Christ?

This is a fraught theological question, one I cannot answer fully here.[32] But we can at least say, with C. S. Lewis, "If you are a Christian you do not have to believe that all the other religions are simply wrong all through. . . . When I was an atheist I had to try to persuade myself that most of the human race have always been wrong about the question that mattered to them most; when I became a Christian I was able to take a more liberal view."[33] The "more liberal view" is not that all religions are right but that no religion is all wrong. Standing behind every religion, as J. H. Bavinck writes, is "the inexpressible mystery of God's involvement with fallen humanity."[34] Graciously, God is present and at work in every culture and religion of the world, despite every culture and religion's idolatry and injustice.

But what no religion can ever find on its own, no matter how sincere its search, what must burst forth in a special way, is the God-man, Jesus Christ. We can see an acknowledgment of the mystery of God's involvement in the testimony of the apostle Paul at Mars Hill (Acts 17:24–28). There Paul notes the altar dedicated to "the unknown god" and says, "What therefore you worship as unknown, this I proclaim to you." In the course of his recorded remarks, he will engage in iconoclasm, confronting Athenian idolatry ("We ought not to think that the divine being is like gold or silver or stone, an image formed by the art and the imagination of man"). But Paul starts by making a connection: he tells the Athenians that God's purpose in creating, guiding, and governing creation is so that humans "should seek God, in the hope that they might feel their way toward him and find him." He affirms Athenian religion even as he challenges it, quoting their poets Epimenides and Aratus. And even though the passages he cites originally refer to Zeus, Paul says, "They got something right!"[35] This affirmation means that we should expect to find glimmers of glory, not just implicitly in cultural forms but also in explicitly religious forms.

When we treat religion as an element of culture, we can similarly expect to find both cultural wisdom and cultural idolatry. But insofar as religion specializes in the limits of human life—in imagining what is beyond those limits and how we might transcend them—our propensity to go astray is even greater, and far greater dangers await us when we do. Religion is always at risk of becoming a means of self-glorification, justifying the human by manipulating the divine.

This brings me to my final question: If sectarianism is a natural human tendency, doesn't religion supercharge this impulse? If we believe that our religious truth is underwritten by God, what will keep us from triumphalism, or worse? We might notice how often competitive athletes have a strong sense of being chosen by God, making a point of genuflecting, kneeling, or "thanking God" when they win. The tendency shows up in the way they explain their success: an identification of God's mission with their own personal mission. In athletes, such a move may lead to nothing more than an enlarged ego: "God wants me to win." By contrast, the conviction that my ethnic or religious group is *exceptionally* graced is a very dangerous thing. When combined with cultural power, it can justify marginalization, oppression, and even genocide.

This is because "the chosen" usually believe that they earned their election through the purity of their bloodline, military strength, or some other cultural achievement.

To help us resist this, we can turn to another of religion's sharpest critics, Swiss theologian Karl Barth (1886–1968). Barth, like Bonhoeffer, resisted the unholy alliance of religion and regime, authoring much of the Barmen Declaration against Nazism in the German church. This led him to place a strong disjunction between religion and revelation. For Barth, Jesus Christ alone is the revelation of God—revelation's source and substance—God telling us who God is in defiance of human pretensions. By contrast, religion is "unfaithfulness," the human attempt "to justify and sanctify [ourselves] before a willfully and arbitrarily devised image of God." Since religion attempts to know God from its own point of view and with its own resources, it always leads to idolatrous projections. But revelation brings "something utterly new,"[36] something we could not have told ourselves. Revelation is religion's "sublimation," a word that simultaneously means annulment as well as overcoming and fulfillment.[37] We can talk about Christianity as the "true religion," Barth says, but only in the sense that we can talk about a "justified sinner." True religion exists only as "a creature of grace," and thus it is the one thing that no one could ever brag about.[38]

Scripture makes it clear that there can be no boasting in grace as if it were our possession, trophy, or achievement. As Paul writes to the cultured Corinthians,

> Brothers and sisters, think of what you were when you were called. Not many of you were wise by human standards; not many were influential; not many were of noble birth. But God chose the foolish things of the world to shame the wise; God chose the weak things of the world to shame the strong. God chose the lowly things of this world and the despised things— and the things that are not—to nullify the things that are, so that no one may boast before him. It is because of him that you are in Christ Jesus, who has become for us wisdom from God—that is, our righteousness, holiness and redemption. Therefore, as it is written: "Let the one who boasts boast in the Lord." (1 Cor. 1:26–31)

God's grace has nothing to do with our virtue, the location of our birth, or the status of our family. It comes to us when we least expect it and least deserve it. Those who boast must boast in the Lord, not in the superiority of our culture or religion.

Indeed, throughout Scripture, grace *reverses* cultural and religious norms, as when God chooses the younger and weaker over the older and stronger, announces the incarnation to shepherds, or chooses women as the first preachers of the resurrection. God has always reserved the right to decide who God's people will be, and this means that God is free to invite the most unlikely candidates to join God's people and participate in God's kingdom. As Virgilio Elizondo writes, "What humans reject, God chooses as his own."[39] Even Israel—the one group that could ostensibly claim some sort of exceptionalism—is reminded, "It was not because you were greater than all other people that the LORD loved you and chose you. In fact, you were the smallest of peoples! No, it is because the LORD loved you" (Deut. 7:7–8 CEB). Grounded in the unfathomable wisdom of God, grace dissolves all human self-congratulation. If embracing the gospel leads us to pride and presumption rather than awestruck humility and love, then we have not really grasped it. Grace should lead to amazement; it surprises and subverts human pride because it is unconditional, unbuyable, and unexpected from the standards of human ingenuity.

Who could have imagined that God's gift would be God? Augustine made this point eloquently, noting that ancient philosophers pictured a remote perfect being, unmoved by humanity, but also an image of the best of humanity: a rational soul. The poets, by contrast, imagined the gods as immoral and capricious, just like humans at their worst. Through their poetry, they were trying to bring the gods down to earth. But through their highest imaginings, neither the poets nor the philosophers had been able to grasp the divine. The solution to the ancient quarrel between the sacred and the profane, between heaven and earth, was the incarnation: God came down, lived, died, and rose again to reconcile heaven and earth.[40]

This will be the climax of Paul's message at the Areopagus too: "In the past God overlooked such ignorance, but now he commands all people everywhere to repent. For he has set a day when he will judge the world with justice by the man he has appointed. He has given proof of this to everyone by raising him from the dead" (Acts 17:30–31). It is not just that God made the world and continues to be present, shining through the cracks in human culture. Amid our stumbling in the darkness, the Light of life has come down looking for us. God's glory shines most fully in the face of Christ; therefore, all revelation, if it is revelation, may not immediately be related to Christ, but it will invariably pull us toward him. True religion cannot come *from* us; it cannot be the achievement of human spirit, imagination, or culture. It must come *to* us, a gift of the Holy Spirit. Only then can it stand against us in transformative challenge; only then can it stand with us in saving solidarity.

Distinctive Practice: Directional Discernment

This brings us to our distinctive practice: directional discernment. Discernment is a process of asking careful questions to distinguish the directions in which a person or culture is moving, toward and away from God. I am drawing this idea from J. H. Bavinck, who emphasized that the formal study of a religion is not sufficient, since each person's lived experience of a religion may differ from official dogma. The desire for connection—with others and with God—in ways that transcend our individual limitations is a response to revelation that Bavinck calls "communion." "Religion is by its very nature a communion, in which man answers and reacts to God's revelation. . . . Religion can be a profound and sincere seeking of God, [but] it can also be a flight from God, an endeavor to escape from His presence, under the guise of love and obedient service."[41] There is a way of being religious that responds to revelation by fleeing God's presence, by using "God," as it were, to avoid God. But there is also a way of being religious that seeks true communion, listening, receiving, and responding to God's initiating action (a sign that the Holy Spirit is at work). Thus, we must always ask, "What is this person doing inwardly with God?"[42]

We can extend Bavinck's question to cultural practices, movements, and institutions, provided we do not leave individual persons behind. For if the essence of community is to hold something in common, then the character of a community—religious or otherwise—will be the nature of what is shared. Cultural discernment requires distinguishing the directions in which these common things orient us, what a culture or community is doing inwardly with God. No religious practice should escape our careful suspicion, and no religious practice should elicit our callous scorn. For within every religious community and practice we find a yearning both to flee God and to find God.

Here we can return to a primary claim of this book: fulfillment, not replacement. What does this mean when it comes to religion, especially given the human penchant for idolatry? What I mean by "fulfillment" is not that human cultures get us part of the way—say, 30 or 40 or 60 percent—and then the gospel comes in to finish the job. Religion does not point the way to Christ; only the gospel can do that. But the Spirit can prepare hearts through the wrestling of religion, opening spaces, offering cries for something more. The gospel does not cancel such cries; it fulfills them.

We still find ourselves in God's world, a world in which we cannot help but deem things sacred. We might say that this sensitivity reflects a dim recognition of the dignity of God's creatures and the call to handle them with love. For it is *love*, not death, that dignifies life. It is the love that is shared within and among communities of care that points to and participates in the love that God has for creation.

Perhaps, on this side of things, we can never fully escape the possible critique that we may be merely projecting our best ideas about God onto reality. But the real life, death, and resurrection of Jesus Christ gives us strong hope that our deepest desires are not lies and that the world is truly meaningful, moved by "the Love that moves the sun and the other stars."[43] It is because we have this hope that we can continue exploring our imaginings, interrogating our desires, and playing with possibilities. This brings us, in the next chapter, to a discussion of the aesthetic dimension of culture.

QUESTIONS FOR REFLECTION AND DISCUSSION

1. What is a piece of art or popular culture that has really mattered to you, changing your mind about something important, offering solace in a difficult time, helping you connect with a loved one, and so on? What is it about that piece of culture that resonated with you?

2. What are some other nontraditional communities of belonging that function religiously (providing meaning, community, purpose, and ritual)? Is there a

group you have experienced that feels more like a church (or what church is meant to be)?

3. What do you make of the sociological account of religion, which is more about belonging than believing? Do you agree that religion "intensifies" culture? What are the ways that religion has been used throughout history to legitimize the social order? What are the ways you see this happening now?

4. What do you make of the disjunction between religion and revelation? Should we call Christianity a religion? The "true religion"? How do Christians avoid the attendant danger of triumphalism that could result from believing that the Christian account of reality is true?

5. What does the practice of directional discernment look like in everyday life? When we ask, "What is this person doing inwardly with God?" or "What is this community doing inwardly with God?" how does this shift our approach to religion?

THE AESTHETIC DIMENSION

Culture as Poetic Project

The animated movie *Toy Story* imagines the social life of a group of toys. Early in the film, one of the toys—Potato Head—rearranges his facial features: "Look, I'm Picasso!" His friend Hamm—a piggy bank—replies, "Uh . . . I don't get it," and walks away. This leads Potato Head to shout, "You uncultured swine!"[1] The scene makes us laugh, even as it displays a common conception of what it means to be "cultured." Hamm's lack of culture is revealed by his inability to appreciate the finer things in life. Through a failure of effort or education, he remains a humble Hamm, uncultured and uncouth.

Of course, if "getting" modern art is the mark of a cultured person, many will join Hamm in failing the test, which trades on a well-worn distinction between "high culture" and "popular culture." Popular culture has been watered down for the sake of broad appeal and thus represents and reinforces the status quo. By contrast, high culture ennobles us, elevating us to a higher plane. Artifacts of high culture (like Picasso's paintings) refine our tastes, in part by making us work to appreciate them. In keeping with this sensibility, it is common for cinephiles to turn up their noses at hit "movies" (meant to be consumer products) as compared to more highbrow "films" (meant to be works of art). The

2019 blockbuster *Avengers: Endgame* grossed around $3 billion, topping all-time lists as one of the most successful movies ever made. And it is largely because of its commercial triumph that the cultural critics at one magazine ranked it dead last out of over five thousand films made in the 2010s. More like a "ride" than a film, to these reviewers, it encompassed everything that is wrong with popular cinema.[2]

Whether we consider this judgment to be sophisticated or snobbish, it displays what we might call a classical understanding of culture. Cultured people immerse themselves in classic works of art, literature, and music, representing great achievements of the human spirit. These touchstones of creativity provoke us and inspire us; they disclose something important about the mystery of existence. We return to them again and again, and each time they reward us with stories worth retelling, songs worth repeating, poems worth reciting. Classics invite us to inhabit the *aesthetic* dimension of culture, what the poet T. S. Eliot had in mind when he said, "Culture may be defined as that which makes life worth living."[3]

Of the five dimensions of culture that this book explores, the aesthetic is the most difficult to define. Whether we are trying to describe beauty or define art, finding a comprehensive account would betray the subject matter. The meaning of aesthetic artifacts is not reducible to an explanation, as if expounding a poem were equal to hearing it read, or describing a painting were equal to standing in front of it.[4] Here the deepest things can only be found through attention to the surface. The color of the car matters. The elegance of the (Mac) computer matters. The way the chairs are arranged matters. The typeface in the presentation matters. The order of the words matters. The meaning is felt before it is named, and the "felt qualities" are essential to what is meaningful.[5]

Even if we cannot precisely define it, we can still get a sense of what this dimension entails. In this chapter, I will highlight *imaginative generativity* as fundamental to aesthetics. For though we did not choose the stage on which we have been thrown, we almost always seek to make it better and more beautiful.[6] We use our imaginations to reinterpret and renew cultural materials, playing with possibilities, provoking desire and delight. The aesthetic dimension captures the way our culture making becomes *poetic*, as we configure words, images, sounds, scenes, and objects with nuance and symbolic intention. Some are more skilled at this than others. But aesthetic play—found in doodling as surely as in dance—is fundamental to our humanity.

Here there is a clear connection with the religious dimension discussed in the previous chapter. Art has long been a surrogate for religious faith because of the transcendence it triggers and the community it creates.[7] Aesthetic pursuits can be taken extremely seriously, becoming matters of ultimate concern and outright idolatry. Understanding one dimension may help us understand the other. Both dimensions deem spaces, events, people, and objects as "special." A loaf of bread and a glass of wine on my kitchen table are not equal to the consecrated elements of the Communion table. Likewise, a banana duct-taped to my office wall is not the same as the art piece *Comedian*, a banana taped to a gallery wall by Italian artist Maurizio Cattelan.

But *Comedian* also illustrates one reason why the religious and aesthetic aspects of culture must be distinguished: the aesthetic must retain the sense of play (which includes frivolity, triviality, and irony) that is so essential for imaginative making. We need freedom to try out new arrangements and experiment with new approaches, just because it gives us delight. Thus, to encompass both superficiality and depth, I will take the aesthetic dimension to refer to the layer of culture in which we play with possibilities. Sometimes this simply means blowing bubbles or building sandcastles. Other times it means telling stories or painting pictures, pushing the boundaries with artistic flourish. Still other times it means forging rich symbolic systems, even creating imaginative worlds. After surveying the contours of an aesthetic approach to culture, I will situate the conversation between two theological pairs: (1) desire and delight and (2) escape and eschaton. I will call the interpretive practice that emerges from the discussion "generous making."

Aesthetics Broadly Considered: Beauty, Art, and the Play of Imagination

Why do certain things elicit our desire and delight? Is it all relative, a reflection of cultural conditioning? Or is it normative, the proper response to something real? As Prince Charming asked Cinderella in the Rodgers and Hammerstein musical, "Do I love you because you're beautiful? Or are you beautiful because I love you?"[8] Although this is not something I recommend saying to a love interest, Prince Charming asks an important aesthetic question: Does my attraction tell me something about the thing I am seeing? Or does it only tell me something about myself?

The classical understanding is that beauty *inheres* in objects: it is a feature of a world external to our senses, meant to evoke our desire toward the Good. Because reality is of a single piece, the beauty of one part propels us up the "ladder of love" toward its source. In Plato's *Symposium*, the wise woman Diotima argues that loving a beautiful person's body should lead you to love all beautiful bodies. For it is not *this body* you love but the *beauty* that you find there. The love of beautiful bodies should lead to the love of beautiful souls, since such inner beauty is more substantial, remaining after bodily beauty fades. This in turn should lead you to love beautiful societies, which are composed of laws and customs that produce beautiful souls. And finally, you will realize that what you have been loving all along is Beauty itself, the ideal from which all beautiful things draw their brilliance. There is no better life, Diotima says, than one spent in pursuit of the Beautiful.[9]

For thinkers like Plato, beauty was evident in symmetry and synchronicity, in health and harmony, in the elegance of an order that could not help but please human perception. But it is also important to say that beauty *happens* because ordinary things are permeated by invisible realities. The classical idea of a "great chain of being"—in which lower things draw their meaning from higher forms—was transposed into a Christian key by the early church fathers and reached new heights in medieval philosophy.[10] Human desire and delight were understood to be grounded in God, the source of every good thing. Thus, Aquinas can answer Prince Charming's question confidently: "Something is not beautiful because we love it, but rather do we love it, because it is beautiful."[11] We are right to love beautiful things, because they are lovely. They pull us toward the Love that moves the stars and gives music to the spheres.

In the disenchanting environment of early modernity, however, a shift began to occur. Increasingly occupied with perception itself, and less sure about invisible realities, the emphasis shifted from the Beautiful to the Sublime, "the experience of the ineffable and overwhelming."[12] In a disenchanted world, we still have aesthetic experiences that evoke our desire and delight, even to the point of being overwhelmed. But modern interest is increasingly directed from without to within, to what the experiences can tell us about ourselves: our personal or cultural psyche. Modern people tend to be suspicious about claims that any aesthetic "order" exists. It makes more sense to say that our desire and delight are socially constructed, and to repeat the old chestnut about beauty being in the eye of the beholder.

But a sentiment nearer to the truth is often attributed to another "cultured swine," Miss Piggy of Muppets fame. "Beauty is in the eye of the beholder," she says, "and it may be necessary from time to time to give a stupid or misinformed beholder a black eye." This humorous take captures two conflicting intuitions about aesthetic judgments. The first of these is that taste is subjective, reflecting our upbringing, personality, and cultural location. What one person finds delightful, another may disdain. We desire and delight in the things that "fit" us. And so, it is no surprise that what one culture finds appealing (say, Mongolian throat singing or bikini bathing suits), another culture finds strange, off-putting, or obscene.

But the other half of Miss Piggy's statement contains a rival intuition, since it also seems like common sense to say that some people are simply more beautiful than others, that some cultural artifacts are just better than others, and if you can't see the difference, you are the one with the problem. Not everything is equally worthy of our attention, and we know it. Even Scottish philosopher David Hume, who argued that "beauty is no quality in things themselves," also insisted that anyone who tries to compare a hack writer to Milton (the great English poet) is like a person who declares "a pond as wide as the Atlantic."[13] The point is that when we describe a person as beautiful, or a piece of art as exceptional, we feel that there must be some force to our judgments: that others *should* agree with our assessment! We are aware that others disagree, but we feel that if we let them say, "That's just like your opinion, man,"[14] it somehow betrays what we have seen. Like Miss Piggy, we are prepared to *fight* for our judgments of cultural worth, at least with words, if not with fists.

In one of my classes, a favorite discussion revolves around "the most beautiful trash can." I show students four different candidates. The first is sleek and silver, elegant in its form and simple in its utility (the Platonic form of the trash can if there ever was one). The second is hidden within a kitchen counter, emerging at a forty-five-degree angle to facilitate efficient disposal. The third is covered in floral patterns, displaying an excess of color and design. The fourth has been cleverly painted to resemble the beloved cartoon character SpongeBob SquarePants. Students divide evenly between these camps and become animated as they argue for why each trash can should be preferred. Some point out the simple elegance of the first can; others, the unity of form and function in the second can; still others, the gratuitous flourish in the third can; and still others, the delightful ingenuity of the fourth can. The point of the discussion is not so much to decide, once and for all, which trash can is the best, as to notice the ways that form, cultural values of functionality, and historical nostalgia shape our aesthetic judgments.

Yet despite differences in judgment, some cultural artifacts (like the works of William Shakespeare) seem to have stood the test of time, with appreciation increasing the more widely they are distributed. This broad recognition across time and space implies a deficiency in those who fail to see their value. As with food, artistic appreciation requires a refined appetite, the ability to notice all the nuances. Hume argues that due to lack of practice or implicit prejudice (e.g., not giving something a chance because it's not familiar or relevant to your life), most people are not good judges of aesthetic excellence and are thus unqualified to give an opinion.[15] He recommends the cultivation of unprejudiced observers, critics whose judgments of taste can be trusted, regardless of cultural location.

The Aesthetic Instinct: An Adaptive Account

But this does not answer the question of *why* aesthetic objects command our recognition. How can we maintain that art is more than a social construction and thus can transcend culture (aesthetic normativity) without recourse to the Greek ladder of love (where beauty overflows from Being) or to the Christian book of creation (where creation is beautiful because it is God's handiwork)? A common route is to suggest that we have been hardwired for aesthetic experience by adaptive challenges in our prehistoric past. Art philosopher Denis Dutton points to studies that show a remarkable consistency across cultures in what is considered an ideal landscape: open, green space, with water and low-branching trees. It is not for nothing that calendar art, public parks, and golf courses continue to reproduce these features. Each of these elements would have been attractive, Dutton maintains, to the hunter-gatherer way of life. Trees provide the possibility of food and shelter from predators; open space suggests habitable land to be explored; water is life. Atavism (the vestiges of survival instincts) thus accounts for our predilection for natural beauty.[16] To put it differently, we are primed to find aesthetic pleasure in scenes that offer us "a spacious place" (Ps. 31:8), where there is a greater likelihood that we can thrive.

For Dutton, sexual selection explains another key component of the aesthetic instinct: our appreciation of "virtuoso displays." He makes this argument with reference to the first known aesthetic artifact: the Acheulian hand axe, distributed throughout what is now Africa, Europe, and Asia and dating back at least a million years. These elegant implements are noted for their symmetry, teardrop design, and meticulous craftsmanship. And yet they show no sign of practical use. Why make them? The reason, Dutton argues, is that their production sent "fitness signals" to females: intelligence, fine motor control, access to rare materials. Dutton puts it wryly: "Why don't you come up to my cave so I can show you my hand axes?" In our later ancestors, this impulse toward virtuoso display develops into a social practice of using flair and technique to amuse and amaze. The adaptive result, Dutton says, is that humans innately "find beauty in something done well."[17]

This brief sampling does not do justice to Dutton's theory, still less to other evolutionary accounts of the art instinct. It is likely that people will find explanatory power in these accounts to the degree that they are persuaded by the overall Darwinian scheme. In any case, there is a difference between accounting for aesthetic impulses in adaptive terms and giving a wholly adequate account of them. It is not quite clear how we move from what is "agreeable" (where pleasurable sensations are connected to survival instinct) to what is "beautiful" (worthy of sustained contemplation for its own sake). Adaptive explanations should not be used to diminish the complexity of poetic making ("Oh, so that's all it is!"). There is a numinous excess to artistic displays among Homo sapiens, to say the least, and we will return to this in a moment.

I find Dutton's account intriguing for two reasons. First, it seeks an account of aesthetic universality, our intuition that our aesthetic judgments have normative force ("Everyone should appreciate this!"). Second, it taps into a key insight, one also found in Diotima's speech: that aesthetics is connected to *generativity*. Diotima maintains that just as bodily beauty produces generative desire (the begetting of children), so too higher forms of beauty give birth to generative virtue (the begetting of wisdom). Aesthetic experience leads to replication, reproduction, and reinterpretation. We wish a moment could last forever; we share our pictures, paint a likeness, write a song; we are inspired to make something new because of what we have seen. Rather than enclosing us in desire, beauty opens us up to new possibilities. The point, which we could draw either from Diotima's ancient account or from Dutton's modern one, is that beauty is generative. The aesthetic impulse seeks a fruitful space in which all sorts of beautiful things can bloom.

From Discerning Beauty to Creating Art

Perhaps generativity can offer a thread between the ancient fascination with beauty and the modern interest in art. Modern critics complain that beauty is bougie, too idealized and narrow to capture what artists are trying to accomplish. Think of Picasso's *Guernica*, which he painted after the bombing of a Spanish town that killed mostly women and children. Notable for the surreal images of agony it contains, Picasso's painting did not aim to unveil beautiful forms; the images are unpleasant, even jarring. Rather, *Guernica* seeks to make visible what is invisible in society, producing a visceral response in the viewer. In keeping with this sensibility, it is the *social* function of art that tends to dominate contemporary discussions.

Nevertheless, the question remains: Why do certain cultural artifacts become pieces of art? What makes art, art? Some have suggested that art is governed by intention, as when artists self-consciously draw attention to their craft. Others have suggested that art is defined by expression, the making visible of an artist's inner life. Still others highlight the contemplative value of art, over against its social utility: art's sole purpose is to be perceived. Finally, art has an institutional element: it is defined by its recognition as art by the "art world." All these options narrow art's scope to a meaningful range and acknowledge artistic expertise. But they can also seem arbitrary, situated by powerful interests, leaving most of us ill-equipped to acknowledge unfamiliar excellence.

Indeed, when it comes to accounting for aesthetic desire and delight, excellence and elegance can only take us so far. There is another element, much more subjective, yet most undeniably real. There is an *electricity* to aesthetic experience: when an encounter crackles with a connection we cannot quite explain. When discussing the paleolithic paintings from the Chauvet Cave, documentary filmmaker Werner Herzog marvels that the cave paintings have no clear evolutionary precedent. Rather, they seem to have "burst onto the scene like a sudden explosive event."[18] The film explores the numinous power that the paintings seem to exert, leading one scientist to withdraw from the project temporarily, overwhelmed by the experience. Is it the strangeness of the ancient art that is so astounding? Why then does it feel so familiar, across all boundaries of time and place? Reflecting on the remains of a Greek sculpture, the poet Rainer Maria Rilke felt a claim on his entire existence: "You must change your life."[19]

How do we account for this sort of astonishment? For artist and philosopher J. F. Martel, mystery is at the very heart of the aesthetic experience: "Art is the name we have given to humanity's most primal response to the mystery of existence. It was in the face of the mystery that dance, music, poetry, and painting were born."[20] We can note the religious overtones in this definition, and Martel (who is not a theist) frequently uses religious categories in describing art. He even frames his project in terms of religious iconoclasm, naming and negating *pornography* and *propaganda* as two "golden calves" that have taken art's place. Martel has in mind not just internet sites or cable news but any use of aesthetics that seeks to manipulate through desire (pornography) or fear (propaganda). Such manipulations turn *art* into artifice: rather than arresting our attention in revelatory encounter, artifice tells us all the answers, what to do, and whom to hate.[21] The peddlers of pornography and propaganda know that desire directs human action, and so they seek to take it captive. But in so doing, they rob the world of mystery and neuter art's power. They cannot offer us anything new; they can only endlessly repackage what we already know.

The aesthetic dimension thus offers a bulwark against the tendency of the power dimension to overreach in its approach to culture. Against the masters of suspicion, artists remind us that the rich intricacies of human culture making cannot be reduced to economics, sex, or power. If political ideologies tend to take generative symbols from the aesthetic realm and turn them into instruments of their agendas, great art resists this reduction. Aesthetics protects culture from political captivity by holding space for new configurations, pondering possibilities that endanger the structures of coercive power. Art offers the possibility to transcend "tribal norms," crossing boundaries and cultivating empathy across deep difference.[22]

From Artistic Creation to Imaginative Play

Martel's "Romantic" account of art (in which wonder fuels artistic creation) captures something important about the aesthetic dimension. It is common to consider contemplation to be the root not just of art but of culture itself.[23] But I wonder if this makes aesthetics too much a matter of "magic," or at least mystical experience. Perhaps this is an unsurprising outcome if art is asked to step in for religion, to communicate the transcendence and awe once felt in response to the divine.

But we should be careful not to confuse religion and art, reducing one to the other, or expecting epiphanic experience to explain either dimension of culture. Aesthetics permeates life in much more ordinary ways. Few of us have such visionary experiences; still fewer engage in visionary artistic creation. Yet all of us exercise aesthetic imagination in the activities of everyday life. We sing in the shower. We whistle while we work. We design beautiful spaces in which we feel at home. "A good deal of art," writes Nicholas Wolterstorff, "is to ennoble some humble act that we could perform without the artistic enhancement."[24]

And then there are times when we simply play. In this, children can become our best teachers. They know that play is fundamental. On a hike we arrive at a hidden body of water. Instinctively, my son and daughter begin hunting for rocks. "Do you think I can get it to skip three times?" they ask. Next, they devise a game where we try to throw the rocks as close to the shore as possible without hitting the water (so as not to disturb the fish). The more time we have, the more complex our games can become, adapting to whatever space we find ourselves in and whatever materials are at hand. When I was growing up, we developed a kind of cul-de-sac "baseball" for four players. The pitcher, who also played second base, bounce-pitched a tennis ball from that position toward the batter. Another team member played all the outfield positions.

Any ball hit in the air past the fourth mailbox was a home run. Why did we wake up every day, ready to play again, always seeking to fine-tune the game? Why do adults still seek out, participate in, and fanatically follow so many varieties of play? We do it because generative play is a vital part of being human.[25]

As a human phenomenon, play will always be fraught with human frailty. Play may lose its joy in cutthroat competition, as when a friendly softball game becomes an exercise in ego. It may become a means of establishing hierarchy of persons or eras (who is the GOAT?). As play becomes more complex, it may become commodified by corporate interests seeking to enrich themselves by building a brand. It may become an arm of civil religion or a space for civil disobedience. As with art, powerful interests seek to leverage play as a tool for directing desire. Just as art can become advertisement or amusement, delight can give way to distraction or addiction. In such cases, imaginative play gets disoriented toward self-serving pursuits that diminish our common humanity.

And yet, none of these complicating factors disqualify the primal human impulse to play. We might even say that robust imaginative play is a key indicator of our ability to thrive. Development workers report that the health of refugee settlements can often be evaluated by how children play in the camps. As William Dyrness writes, "In the worst situations, children no longer play but walk or lie listlessly about. In healthier places, children laugh and run about. Children's play becomes the canary in the coal mine—that is the marker able to depict the presence or absence of justice."[26] If there is space to engage in the free exercise of imagination—not for any particular purpose other than for the joy of play—then other imaginings, innovations, and hopes are also possible.[27] Aesthetic generativity can tell us something about the health of a culture.

To summarize: the aesthetic dimension is a layer of cultural life in which we—with desire and delight—play with the possibilities of life in this world. This dimension seeks a generative space to flourish, with as much freedom as possible from mercenary manipulations of desire. But what constitutes generativity? And what are the limits that keep delight from becoming distraction, desire from becoming obsession? To answer these questions, we need theological resources to help us place the aesthetic impulse within the imaginative universe of Scripture. How are desire and delight directed by the biblical story? And how might they anticipate the fulfillment of human culture making in the age to come?

Theological Thread 1: Desire and Delight

Theology is often oriented around the events of redemptive history—God's action to heal fallen creation—and rightly so. But Scripture invites us to consider not just the *telos* of the world (the direction the story is moving) but also its *texture* (the place where it is set). It supplies us with a body of literature marked by attention to the details of human experience: the Wisdom books. Psalms, Proverbs, Ecclesiastes, Song of Songs, and Job stand out in the canon for their allusivity. These books begin, not with the big story of creation, fall, and redemption, but with the human search for wisdom. This search takes place in a world filled with delight and doxology but also danger and disorientation. The sages ask, What is this place? What is worth holding on to? What does it mean to live well?

Let us begin with their delight. Concerned as they are with concrete realities, it is no surprise that the Wisdom books are full of aesthetic attention. Consider the inspired utterance of Agur, son of Jakeh:

> There are three things that are too amazing for me,
>   four that I do not understand:
> the way of an eagle in the sky,
>   the way of a snake on a rock,
> the way of a ship on the high seas,
>   and the way of a man with a young woman. (Prov. 30:18–19)

The sages marvel at insight gained from carefully observing the world. Convinced that the world belongs to God, they look for wisdom anywhere it can be found, believing that rocks, plants, birds, and ants can be our teachers. It is also notable that Agur is not an Israelite. With the inclusion of his words, we find wisdom originating outside the covenant community, recognized as having the ring of truth.[28] To be sure, every proverb is organized under "the fear of Yahweh," which is the beginning of wisdom (Prov. 1:7). But this fundamental posture of reverence enhances the ability of the sages to appreciate the created world and its creative humans, even to hear God's voice in what they find. Far from

causing us to discount these works, the fear of the Lord gives us even
more reason to pay attention, while also offering criteria (e.g., righteousness and justice) for discerning between the many occasions for delight
we may find (Prov. 9).

Wisdom literature also abounds with desire, both frustrated and fulfilled. "The LORD is my shepherd" (Ps. 23:1) sits side by side with "My
God, my God, why have you forsaken me?" (Ps. 22:1). The sages affirm
the goodness of the material world: the sun singing out of a clear sky
(Ps. 19), the electric charge of erotic love (Song of Songs), the way that
God has "made everything beautiful in its time" (Eccles. 3:11). But they
also wrestle with the absurdity of injustice, the burden of growing old,
and the way that everything slips through our fingers like smoke. They
acknowledge the flies in the ointment, the loose threads, the ill-fitting
fragments of life. As they struggle to make sense of the world, the Wisdom writers frequently challenge the structures of belief that are taken
for granted, and they display an openness to new possibilities. We can see
this in David's songs of lament, Job's dialogue with his friends, and the
Preacher's questioning of everything "under the sun." Walter Brueggemann argues that Wisdom literature confronts "common theology, which
assumes predictable, even contractual results," that we will always reap
what we sow.[29] Things are not so simple: "The race is not to the swift or
the battle to the strong, nor does food come to the wise or wealth to the
brilliant or favor to the learned; but time and chance happen to them
all" (Eccles. 9:11). And yet, while the Wisdom writers may question the
mystery of the world and the justice of God, they also ultimately find
their home in God's loyal love.

The Wisdom books offer vital resources for directing our aesthetic
delight and desire, especially in cultures that grant aesthetics pride of
place. As Charles Taylor has argued, Westerners have long been living
in an "age of authenticity," where we *feel* our way forward, convinced
that reality must be resonant with our felt experience. The implications
of this aesthetic shift are complicated, to say the least, and Christians
continue to wrestle with the implications for faith, witness, and public
life.[30] One undeniable side effect of the triumph of aesthetics is that we
find ourselves caught in a "hurricane of desire," buffeted by the wind
like the sinners in Dante's second circle of hell.[31] Disordered delight
leads to distraction (the desire for ever novel amusements), addiction

(the inability to turn away), and despair (the result of an "ever increasing craving for an ever diminishing pleasure").[32]

But the created structure of human desire is good, reflecting our hunger to be rightly related to reality. In our fallen condition, our desires require something more than either gratification or renunciation. They require redirection, as the Holy Spirit weaves them into a larger story. God's triune nature reminds us that God is both the ultimate source and the goal of human longing. Sarah Coakley's summary is worth reading slowly: "God the 'Father,' in and through the Spirit, both stirs up, and progressively chastens and purges, the frailer and often misdirected desires of humans, and so forges them, by stages of sometimes painful growth, into the likeness of his Son. . . . In God, 'desire' of course signifies no *lack*—as it manifestly does in humans. Rather it connotes the plenitude of longing love that God has for God's own creation and for its full and ecstatic participation in the divine trinitarian life."[33] Coakley's point is that human desire reaches out in response to God's attention toward us. As the great lion Aslan says to Jill in *The Silver Chair*, "You would not have called to me unless I had been calling to you."[34] In our damaged state of sin, our reach exceeds our grasp. And so, our desires and delights must be refined by the Spirit, who groans within us until we are conformed to the likeness of the Son (Rom. 8:22–27), until we want what Jesus wants. Coakley writes that our desires must be brought, through prayer, into the presence of God, where the Spirit nudges them in new directions. Indeed, for Coakley, worship is essential in the human search for wisdom: "If one is resolutely not engaged in the practices of prayer, contemplation, and worship, then there are certain sorts of philosophical insight that are unlikely, if not impossible."[35]

This is where the Wisdom writers want to take us, situating our desire and delight within the vocation of all creatures, great and small: "Let everything that has breath praise the LORD" (Ps. 150:6). Doxology gives direction to our desire and our delight; in worship, they both find their home. What matters is not aesthetic *experience* but aesthetic *response*: not just encountering beauty but making a beautiful life, in response to the beautiful God.

Here we must take the aesthetic attitude beyond awe at the mystery of existence. Job marveled that we have only seen the edges of God's ways in the mysteries of creation (Job 26:14). But in Jesus Christ we have seen the Creator's face, the one in whom all things hold together (Col. 1:17). This does not remove our astonishment at the mystery; it gives it definite content and concrete direction—to use our creativity as those formed by the Spirit after the likeness of Christ. The Spirit transposes aesthetic wonder into ecstatic worship, without leaving our humanity behind. Calvin Seerveld puts it this way: "What counts is whether or not the look and hearing, the feeling, thinking and human response to the sights and noises and daily miracles levels pride, builds up Christ's body, and stewardly compounds the praise and thanksgiving of God's myriad creatures under our hands and attention."[36] This is the kind of generativity that Scripture says is our birthright: the generativity of grace, the kind that begins in wonder and ends in worship.

Indeed, the surplus of meaning that we find in the aesthetic realm—exceeding our ability to encompass it—is fitting if the world is characterized not by emptiness but by divine extravagance. Another way of saying this is that aesthetics deals in the realm of gratuity: not the gratuity of self-indulgence (the kind found in gratuitous violence or nudity) but the gratuity of grace. Both a child who pushes another off a bicycle and a child who gives away his bicycle do something that is unnecessary, uncalled for. When asked why they did what they did, both will say, "I just wanted to do it." The first child does it "just for the hell of it," while we might say that the second does it "just for the heaven of it."[37]

"Just for the heaven of it" brings together the telos and texture of the aesthetic dimension. God enjoys and inspires beautiful things because they are beautiful. But they are also beautiful because they reflect God's character, as well as the kind of place that God is making the world to be. The generative response to this gratuity, issuing forth in the best of human culture, will endure into the age to come, when "the kings of the earth will bring their glory" into the new Jerusalem (Rev. 21:24 ESV). If this grand vision strains the imagination, we can take a different image of Jerusalem healed, from the prophet Zechariah: "And the streets of the city shall be full of boys and girls playing in its streets" (Zech. 8:5 ESV).

This means we should make no apology for the great many things we do for the sheer joy we find in them. Joy, we recall, is one of the supreme marks of the kingdom (along with righteousness and peace). Why do we laugh? Why do we blow bubbles? Why do we build sandcastles? The answer to all these questions is the same: just for the heaven of it. For the sheer delight of finding a rare stamp, the recognition of an elegant line on the chessboard, the pleasure of fitting a dovetail joint with near-perfect precision. Lifelong learners will speak about the deep satisfaction found in the process of understanding—not because it earns higher marks or sets you apart from your peers but simply because there is such a thing as "learning something it feels unaccountably good to know."[38] We long to learn, just for the heaven of it.

In an earlier chapter, I explored the way that fear of death distinguishes and drives human culture making. But if there is something beyond the grave, then we should not be surprised to find clues, amid human imaginings, of that coming reality. In Li-Young Lee's poem "From Blossoms," the poet describes the experience of buying a bag of peaches and sinking his teeth into a fruit, aware of the life and labor that has preceded and produced his moment of delight. In such instances of everyday excess, he writes, it is "as if death were nowhere / in the background."[39] Sometimes, in aesthetic delight, we lose sight of death, feeling as if we have escaped the cycles of the earth. Theologically, we can say that this primary posture of delight is in some ways a leaping out of ordinary limits in anticipation of the coming kingdom, the world of joy. To act "just for the heaven of it" connects delight to desire and anticipates a moment when "the door on which we have been knocking all our lives will open at last."[40]

Theological Thread 2: Escape and Eschaton

This brings us to the second theological pair: escape and eschaton. I place these two terms together because thinking about heaven, or eschatology (to use the technical term for the doctrine of last things), is often accused of being escapist. Similarly, the great critique of aesthetics is that it is frivolous, a fixation on the superficial, rather than a reckoning with the deep structures of an unjust world. There is no doubt that both aesthetics and eschatology offer a kind of escape. But much depends on the nature of the escape: whence we are fleeing and where we are finding refuge. Can being heavenly minded as I have described it—doing things just for the heaven of it—enable us to live more fruitfully and faithfully in this time and place? Can attention to aesthetics help us to escape in the right way?

Theologians have long maintained that beauty is a clue of the world that was lost, as well as the world that is to come.[41] They suggest that in art we can catch glimpses of creation healed. Both eschatology and art share the requirement of robust imagination, the ability to envision what others cannot see. To see the nations that once trampled the temple now streaming toward it to worship, to see swords repurposed into plowshares, to see children playing in the streets of a war-torn city—all of these stir up our desire for the renewal of all things.

But it is precisely opposition to such visions of final harmony that leads skeptics to reject the heavenly vision. Critics allege that the hope of "pie in the sky by and by" is little more than a sedative. Since eschatological hope looks toward the future, it undermines action in the present. Others have pointed out the ways that apocalyptic fascination leads to cultural collapse. Believers who are fixated on reading the "signs of the times" withdraw from culture, creating cults. In hopes of ushering in the end times, they may even justify or perpetrate violence. The point is that whenever groups claim to know "in detail how things will turn out," drawing definitive lines around who is in and who is out, the possibilities of creative culture making are paralyzed.[42]

But what if eschatology, like aesthetics, is a "flight to reality" rather than from it? I take this argument from Tolkien's stunning essay "On Fairy Stories," in which he answers the accusation that fantasy literature (characterized by exhaustive world building, invented languages, and magic) is mere escapism. The key to his response is a distinction between two sorts of escape. One sort of escape we should rightly resist: *desertion*, like soldiers who abandon their posts in selfish pursuits. But there is another sort of escape, a heroic motif: escape from unjust imprisonment. He writes, "Why should a man be scorned if, finding himself in prison, he tries to get out and go home? Or if, when he cannot do so, he thinks and talks about other topics than jailers and prison-walls? The world outside has not become less real because the prisoner cannot see it."[43] If we find ourselves in a world evacuated of mystery, then nothing is more fitting than wanting to escape, to go home. Tolkien argues that we are drawn to fairy tales because they cleanse our imagination. They take the familiar features of the world and render them strange, reengaging our attention and, with it, our creative humanity.

Tolkien's final argument, however, is his most significant one. He writes that the heart of the fairy tale is *consolation*, when in the face of countless reasons to despair, Joy breaks through. He even coins a new word, "eucatastrophe" (a good catastrophe), to capture the "sudden joyous 'turn'" that is often felt when we read fairy tales. He writes,

> This joy, which is one of the things which fairy-stories can produce su-premely well, is not essentially "escapist," nor "fugitive." In its fairy-tale—or otherworld—setting, it is a sudden and miraculous grace: never to be counted on to recur. It does not deny the existence of *dyscatastrophe*, of sorrow and failure: the possibility of these is necessary to the joy of deliverance; *it denies (in the face of much evidence, if you will) universal final defeat and in so far is* evangelium *[gospel], giving a fleeting glimpse of Joy, Joy beyond the walls of the world, poignant as grief.*[44]

We long for eucatastrophe, Tolkien believed, because it is woven into the structure of the world. The incarnation is the great eucatastrophe of the human story; the resurrection, the great eucatastrophe of the story of Jesus. Jesus Christ—alive from the dead and returning to make things right—is the Joy on which all other joys hang.

Let us say that the aesthetic dimension reminds us of two important truths about the imagination, eschatological or otherwise. First, even as it awakens our desire, it cautions us against giving in to the premature illusion that we have reached the end of our quest. The most poignant moments of beauty awaken in us a desire for something beyond our imagination (1 Cor. 2:9; Eph. 3:20). The temptation is to think that we have already arrived, that the journey has come to an end. But, as George MacDonald reminds us, "It is only the uncultivated imagination that will amuse itself where it ought to worship and work."[45] We continue our ordinary work, ever open to the subtle touches of Joy that surprise us as we do.

Second, the desire and delight that we encounter in the aesthetic realm also tell us something about the nature of the world. They tell us that delight is not the distraction but the deeper reality. The joy that we find in our hobbies, in friendship, in anything done "just for the heaven of it" is not a lie. It is a fleeting glimpse of "Joy, Joy beyond the walls of the world, poignant as grief." We need the aesthetic dimension to clarify our vision, even as we need the story of the gospel to ground our hopes.

In a fallen world, both beauty and brutality are visceral realities. The struggle is to believe that the beauty is deeper than the brutality. To give in to beauty, even for just a moment, is to give in to hope.

For the "living hope" of Christian faith that "all will be well" is grounded not in the generative capacity of human imagination but in the real body of the risen Christ (1 Pet. 1:3). The gospel is generative, not simply because it contains spiritual truths or points to deeper realities, but because it *happened* in a concrete time and place. It not only points us to a world beyond our senses; it satisfies our senses: "That which was from the beginning, which we have heard, which we have seen with our eyes, which we have looked upon and have touched with our hands, . . . the life was made manifest, and we have seen it" (1 John 1:1–2 ESV).

Later in the same letter, John holds the ambiguous details together with confident hope: "Dear friends, now we are children of God, and what we will be has not yet been made known. But we know that when Christ appears, we shall be like him, for we shall see him as he is. All who have this hope in him purify themselves, just as he is pure" (1 John 3:2–3). What we are now is not what we will be. Whatever that means is a mystery, but we are also assured of continuity. We are told, at least, that we shall be with Christ, and even more, like Christ. Elsewhere, our "glorification" (an audacious word) is compared by biblical authors to the relationship between a seed and the harvest (1 Cor. 15:37). I take this to mean not a replacement of all we have loved and longed for but a transfiguration.

Indeed, perhaps the transfiguration of Jesus offers us the best glimpse of what is coming. The transfiguration anticipates the resurrection of Jesus, which in turn anticipates the restoration of the new creation. It is a down payment on the promise that, as N. T. Wright likes to say, God will do for all of creation what he has done in Jesus. When creation is healed, set free from futility, we too will shine like stars (Matt. 13:43). It is hard to imagine what exactly this could mean. But however we imagine it, we should note that Jesus's transfiguration included his clothing, that bit of human culture, taken up and transposed along with his human body. Jesus does not replace our bodies and human artifacts with something more "spiritual." All these things are taken up and given a greater glory. "What are all these fragments for," writes Marilynne Robinson, "if not to be finally knit up?"[46]

Eschatology, like aesthetics, flourishes in the tension between the now and the not yet. In the Gospel account, Peter is so absorbed by the moment that he offers to build three shelters, one for Moses, one for Elijah, and one for Jesus. And there is something right about Peter's attempt to honor the moment, to prolong it, to enclose it in a tabernacle. But as Peter is speaking, he is interrupted by a voice, telling him to stop talking and to start listening. The point, of course, is that God is building a different sort of shelter for his people, and that there will be no final temple without Jesus's journey to Jerusalem, no theology of glory without a theology of the cross. Disciples cannot stay on the mountaintop. We must watch Jesus walk to the cross and then take up our own crosses too. We are not to speak about the transfiguration until after the resurrection because we cannot understand experience on the mountain until we too have passed through the valley of humiliation, until we too have experienced life on the other side of death.

Distinctive Practice: Generous Making

What do we do while we wait for the renewal of all things? We play with possibilities, cultivating creation in light of what we have seen in the face of Jesus Christ. Here the recognition of God's generosity leads us to gratitude and to generativity. Few have captured this generative impulse as well as cultural critic Lewis Hyde:

> The art that matters to us—which moves the heart, or revives the soul, or delights the senses, or offers courage for living, however we choose to describe the experience—that work is received by us as a gift. Even if we have paid a fee at the door of the museum or concert hall, when we are touched by a work of art something comes to us which has nothing to do with the price. I went to see a landscape painter's works, and that evening, walking among pine trees near my home, I could see the shapes and colors I had not seen the day before. The spirit of an artist's gifts can wake our own. . . . We feel fortunate, even redeemed. . . . When we are moved by art we are grateful that the artist lived, grateful that he labored in the service of his gifts.[47]

Even if a piece of art can be bought and sold, Hyde writes, it is not dependent on the market to exist: "But where there is no gift, there is no art." The aesthetic impulse is kept alive, so to speak, by "constant donation," the desire to keep the gift going, either by returning to it, by sharing it, or by making something our own.

I've noticed something about my children. We have a no-screen-time rule on Sundays, wanting that day to feel different from other days. And almost every Sunday my children *make something*: they come up with songs, Lego masterpieces, or artistic creations. In one case, my son made a suit of Mandalorian armor out of cardboard. It led me to start asking them a question: What did you make today? That's a question we can ask ourselves every day. The temptation in a world gone mad is to stand on the sidelines and point out the problems with everyone and everything. But there is an alternative to this: to criticize by creating. We can write songs, poems, and plays; make short films; record podcasts; and start book clubs and prayer meetings. We can make something that offers a glimpse of how things really are.

Sometimes my students tell me they're not creative. But they're wrong. To be creative—to enter whatever situation we've been given and to make it better—is our birthright as image bearers. And in making, posture is what matters. Either we can pursue originality (trying to do it like no one else has ever done it), or we can pursue obedience (faithfulness to the callings that God has placed on our life). The former leads to hipster elitism, where we are obsessed with being original and authentic; the latter leads to servant creativity, where we are no longer thinking about ourselves at all. May our cultural work be of the latter sort, offered ever in the spirit of God's unspeakable gift.

QUESTIONS FOR
REFLECTION AND DISCUSSION

1. What are some of the ways that the aesthetic impulse manifests itself in your life? Is it primarily through appreciation of excellence/elegance or artistic making, or is it some other way?

2. What are some aesthetic experiences that have moved you deeply? Are there any encounters you've had with a piece of art or culture that made you want to change your life?

3. When it comes to the escapist element of culture, how might we distinguish between "good" escapes and "bad" escapes? How do we know when our enjoyment of cultural artifacts is an escape "from reality" or "to reality"?

4. What are some of the resources that help you navigate what this chapter calls the "hurricane of desire"? Instead of simply gratifying or denying our desires, how might we allow the Scriptures to deepen and direct them?

5. What does it mean to "criticize by creating"? How do you take the elements of ordinary life and seek to make them better and more beautiful? What did you make today?

CONCLUSION

The Lived Dimension—the Difficulties of Doing Cultural Theology

A central image in this book has been a conversation around a shared meal. We could even frame the interpretive practices from each chapter according to the elements of eating together: becoming a host, setting the table, making the food, sharing the meal. For this reason, it is fitting to open this final chapter with a reflection on the most important meal that Christians share: the Lord's Supper.

I was raised in a loving Christian home, and we attended a Baptist church "every time the doors were open" (two services on Sunday and one service on Wednesday). Although in adulthood I found my way into a different Christian stream, I have warm memories of my childhood church. But there was one practice that I now find unusual: we only took Communion once a year. The service was closed to nonmembers, and we were encouraged to come in a spirit of self-examination. Because it was so rare, the service was special, notable for its somberness and silence. It was meaningful in the way that holiday services are meaningful.

Fifteen years after leaving home, I found myself serving on the staff of a Presbyterian church that observed weekly Communion. There I learned a new rhythm of worshiping life, in which the proclamation of the Word was always followed by an invitation to the Lord's Table.

129

I began to experience the Supper as nourishing in a new way. I began to yearn for it, so that a worship service felt incomplete without it, like a call with no response. Communion became a "second sermon." Regardless of how well we pastors preached, the promises of the gospel were always on offer in the bread and cup, "the gifts of God for the people of God."

Among the memorable experiences I had while taking Communion at the church, one story stands out. A friend and fellow church member attended his first service back after the sudden, tragic death of his young wife and unborn daughter. As soon as the elements were offered, he ran down the aisle to be first in line to receive them. I can hardly remember (or recount) the story without tears. Can I ever look at Communion the same way?

In recent years we have moved to a congregation that takes Communion less frequently. The leadership of the church has been contemplating a change for some time, moving toward weekly observance. There has been resistance, and as I've listened to the objections, here is what I've gleaned: For many of my fellow members, the historical experience of Communion has emphasized its penitential nature. The Lord's Supper reminds them of their shortcomings; its prerequisite is intensive self-examination and interpersonal reconciliation. Older members even recall an additional, preparatory service that took place the week prior to Communion observance. The idea of engaging in such rigorous introspection every week—discerning whether they are fit to observe the sacrament—is exhausting. For younger members struggling with faith, it means being faced with a weekly decision: Am I really a Christian? Consequently, Communion is experienced as a rite of exclusion, a demonstration that they are *not* among the faithful who walk forward to express their devotion. Every time the meal is taken, it tells them, "You don't belong." Given these objections—which are felt viscerally, in the bodies of those who express them—it is not surprising that changing the church's practice has taken time. There are imaginative gaps, not just intellectual ones, to be crossed.

My purpose in sharing this personal retrospective is not to argue for a particular frequency of Communion observance among Christians (though I'm sure I've shown my hand). I share it to illustrate the relationship between *practice* (what we do) and *meaning* (how it connects).

Communion gains a special nuance among groups with a common practice; the frequency and manner of the practice alters the meaning of the
meal. It is also clear that whatever we bring to the Table shapes the way
we share it and that having an official interpreter (like a pastor) tell us the
meaning of Communion only accomplishes so much. Some of my fellow
members are worried that the meal will "lose its meaning" if taken every
week. But it is more accurate to say that Communion would become
meaningful in a new way. If taking Communion more frequently renders
it less "special" and more ordinary, it could also make it less occasional
and more central. In any case, our "interpretation" of Communion—
our sense of what it means and why it matters—is bound up in layers of
preunderstanding, personal history, and cultural practice.

But isn't there a meaning for Communion that remains, regardless
of what we make of it? Yes. Scripture tells us that regardless of how we
experience it, regardless of our interpretation, regardless of how we
feel, God promises to meet us at the Table (1 Cor. 11:23–26). We might
call this "authorial intent"—what God means by it—even if that fails to
capture the profundity of God's continuing action. There is something
that the Host intends to accomplish through inviting us to the Table,
and somehow the Spirit makes it so, catching us up into the life and love
of the triune God. This, ultimately, is our hope: God's unspeakable gift
(2 Cor. 9:15). The task of theology is to discern what God is doing, not
apart from human meaning making, but in it and through it.[1] We can
acknowledge all the other layers of meaning that are present and still
experience something of God's gracious intent.

When interpreting our world, the complex interaction of all these
layers should not be obscured. Complexity is present in any act of interpretation; it is the fruit of a multifaceted creation. When compounded by
human creativity, there will always be *more* meaning than we can describe.
Apart from sin, this richness of meaning, this "semantic plenitude" would
be a blessing. But sin now saturates all interpretations, both in what we
perceive and in what we perform, and this means that the gifts of God—in
the church and in culture—will always be blighted as soon as they enter
our hands. Our fallenness does not disqualify their status as gift, nor
does it remove our responsibility to receive them rightly. But it should
make us more willing to entertain complexity, to receive correction, and
to resist triumphalism. As James reminds us, both our propensity for evil

and God's unflinching generosity are reasons to be "quick to listen, slow to speak and slow to become angry" (James 1:13–19).

Given the complexity, this book has sought to offer a non-reductive, non-dismissive, and non-anxious introduction to the conversation between theology and culture. In this concluding chapter, I would like to investigate the claim made in the introduction: "Your interpretation is your life." On the surface, the meaning is plain: whether we are interpreting Scripture or culture, it matters what we *do*, not just what we think, believe, or feel.[2] It is not that clear thinking or correct theology is inconsequential, as if we could reduce interpretation to practice. It is rather that "faith without works is dead" (James 2:26 NET). Both theory and practice inevitably demonstrate our religious orientation, our faith commitments, the places we have put our trust.

But lived interpretation—of scriptural text and cultural context—is also fraught with difficulty. Our approach to Christian practice must retain a healthy respect for the complex ways that theology and culture interact, without losing confidence that God is still at work. To help us with this, we will take a brief foray into the world of liturgical theology (the theology of gathered worship). Indeed, insofar as liturgical theologians seek coherence among practice, experience, and belief, they have much to teach us about discerning God's work amid the "work of the people" (a popular definition of liturgy). From there we will move back outside the walls of the church, with the conviction that there, too, God graciously works.

Learning from Liturgical Theology

Liturgical theology can refer to the theology *of* worship, or to the use of liturgical texts *for* worship, or to the theology implicit *in* the practice of worship. Its central insight is often summarized in the Latin phrase *lex orandi, lex credendi*: "The law of prayer is the law of belief." In other words, worship does not merely express what we believe; what we believe is grounded in the experience of worship. Worship practices shape us in ways that are well-fitting or ill-fitting with the words we profess. Imagine a church that claims to be trinitarian but consistently forgets the Holy Spirit when they gather. Which matters more, their profession or their practice?

Liturgical theology's focus on ritual—the regular habits of worship—parallels contemporary theology's renewed interest in the practices of Christian faith.[3] Philosopher James K. A. Smith brings both together in his "cultural liturgies" project, which evaluates culture through the lens of ritual formation. What if, Smith asks, daily habits form us more powerfully than religious beliefs? What if we participate in "secular liturgies," not just sacred ones? Smith argues that "we are what we love" and that what we love is the result of regular action, habits that point our hearts in particular directions. Many habits we consider trivial, like online shopping, may be thicker than we think; hidden in these practices is a vision of a deeper purpose ("I live to shop"). Everyday regimens of formation work against what we experience when we are in church. This leads to Smith's diagnosis: we may not love what we think we love.[4]

Smith's project extends liturgical theology's conviction that practice shapes belief. It also recalls a common lament by ministers in a media-saturated world: "We only have our people for a couple of hours a week. How can we possibly compete with on-demand entertainment, social media, and cable news?" How indeed? If everyday practices are the true site where spiritual formation (or deformation) occurs, the remedy is to expose secular liturgies, even as we try to renew sacred ones. As Smith writes, "A proper response to this situation is to change our practice—to reactivate and renew those liturgies, rituals, and disciplines that intentionally embody the story of the gospel and enact a vision of the coming kingdom of God in such a way that they'll seep into our bones and become the background for our perceptions, the baseline for our dispositions, and the basis for our (often unthought) action in the world."[5] To renew Christian practice, for Smith, is to reinvigorate the Christian community as a distinctive, countercultural body, one that anticipates the coming kingdom.

There is much to commend in Smith's cultural liturgies project, which is a welcome tonic for overly intellectual accounts of culture (in which culture is composed primarily of ideas, which can be resisted by storing up other ideas). But Smith's analysis also contains a tension common to liturgical theology. In his illuminating essay "Difficulties in Doing Liturgical Theology," Paul Bradshaw shows how the discipline has struggled with two characteristic tendencies.[6] First, in its quest to name universal elements for worship (what should always be done), liturgical theology tends to obscure the diversity of historic Christian practice, designating outlying traditions like my childhood church "catholic exceptions."[7] Second, in its desire to emphasize the work of God (what God is doing), it misses the complexity of meaning making attached to those practices, as well as how they can go astray.

Similarly, it seems to me that we can overemphasize the presence of a single, official meaning to our practices—directing us either to God or idols—which, for good or ill, gets impressed on participants. As Bradshaw points out (drawing from Jewish liturgist Lawrence Hoffman), every ritual contains at least four layers of meaning:

1. *Official* meanings, which represent "the things experts say a rite means"

2. *Private* meanings, which are subjective for each person, signifying "whatever idiosyncratic interpretations people find in things"

3. *Public* meanings, which are held in common by meaningful groups, "shared by a number of ritual participants, even though they are not officially preached by the experts"

4. *Normative* meanings, which capture the way that rituals work their way into everyday life, the "structure of signification that ritual affixes upon the non-ritualized world"[8]

To return to the opening example, the *official* meaning of Communion might be found in a theology textbook or preached from the pulpit. *Private* meanings are held by each person in attendance, dependent on a wide variety of factors. Disparate private meanings may make one person weep when invited to the Table, while making another withdraw to the restroom until it is over. *Public* meanings are shared by groups: perhaps for older members of a particular congregation, the primary meaning of Communion is penitence, while younger members savor the vital connection to something ancient and deep. Finally, the *normative* meaning of Communion impresses itself on the members of the congregation throughout the week, in memory, anticipation, or forgetfulness at other tables and other meals. The point is that the power of practices is found in the way they are taken up by participants, not just in how the meaning of that practice is explained by experts. Although it is tempting to think that the official meaning is the one that matters most, it is the other layers of meaning that often have greater force in the lives of worshipers.[9]

This does not mean that worship is merely "what we make of it," or that theological expertise and exposition are not valuable, or that God's action is at the mercy of human response. But it does mean that it is not a simple thing to delineate the work of the people and the work of God. Certainly, we should strive to fit our worship to the gospel story as best we can; we should believe that God meets us "where two or three gather" (Matt. 18:20). But what is not as certain is that we can fix Christian discipleship simply by attending to Christian practice. Answering the question of how our practices shape us, or how worship works, is a complex, continual process of critical reflection and discernment. I may believe that it is good and right to practice weekly Communion. But I also want to honor my childhood church as more than a "catholic exception," if for no other reason than that my own faith was deeply nourished in that place. It was far from perfect, but I heard the gospel more times than I can count.

What can we learn from liturgical theology about interpreting culture? First, we learn that care is needed in describing how God takes up human cultural action into the divine economy. Rather than diminishing God's action, we need to discern God's action at each layer of meaning making, even as we acknowledge that God is doing more than we can discern. Second, we learn that practice is no panacea. We can't worship or work our way to wholeness without spending significant time exploring the layers of meaning present in our practices. How does God's action connect with, challenge, correct, and complete our official, private, public, and normative meanings?

In the case of Communion, it is significant that the eucharistic elements are the result of human cultivation: bread and wine, not grain and grape.[10] Cultural considerations further situate the sacramental meal: the language that is spoken (Latin? English? bilingual?), the frequency of the meal (weekly? monthly? quarterly?), or the elements that are used (one loaf? gluten-free wafers? unleavened bread? grape juice?). Each of these decisions introduces additional layers of significance, which may amplify or countervail the official meaning of the meal. And yet, amid all of this, we are promised that God meets us at the Table. Human cultural elements and human cultural judgments are taken up by the Spirit to exceed themselves with meaning and presence. This is mysterious, to be sure; the point is faithful participation, not absolute comprehension.

A similar dynamic is at work in all our cultural practices. Aware of our finitude and fallenness, we do our best to offer up the work of our hands to the Lord. And graciously, God meets us as we do, establishing the work of our hands, even transposing it into a nobler key. Scholars like Smith offer incisive readings of the way that secular liturgies pull us toward God or idols. We might call this the "official meaning" of these liturgies, discerned by seasoned cultural exegetes. Such "expert meaning" is often hard-won and battle tested and should not be easily discounted. But the official meaning captures only one element, one of the many directions present in any practice. To use Smith's favorite example, when we visit a shopping mall, it is difficult to discern the impact of the elements that make up the composite experience: marketers who attune consumer desire, architects who create the built environment, storeowners who curate the shopping experience, and the mallgoers who are all pursuing projects of their own.[11] But even if the official meaning of the mall (and the consumerist vision that funds it) is deformative, we experience it within a field of force that also includes public, private, and normative meanings. Our desires are given multiple directions, and not all these directions need be distractions from God.

Consider a father and a son who regularly attend professional football games together. They participate in all the rituals associated with the sport: wearing ceremonial dress (jerseys), arriving early for fellowship with others (tailgating), removing caps to rise and sing the anthem, joining with one voice to perform their loyalty to their team. This a profoundly meaningful, even liturgical event. Perhaps their allegiance is being pushed in the direction of patriotism or even nationalism as the anthem is sung. Perhaps their desires are being trained to love athletic prowess more than humble service. Perhaps their sports obsession distracts them from the work of justice in their community. But none of these elements change the fact that the reason why the games are significant to the father and son is the loving connection they experience when they attend together. This is their "normative" meaning, and it is more important (at least to them) than any glosses given by expert interpreters. Those meanings matter too. But the complexity should chasten any tendency to make cavalier pronouncements on what a cultural practice or artifact means.

In her searching book *The Dangers of Christian Practice*, Lauren Winner shows how Communion, baptism, and prayer have been *deformative* in characteristic ways throughout Christian history. She recounts how medieval Christians fabricated "Host desecration" narratives to justify anti-Semitic violence. She describes how "christening parties" grew up around the practice of baptism, rendering it more of a familial rite than an ecclesial one. She surveys the prayer journals of slave-owning Americans who were blind to their country's most grievous sin. Her point is that there is no such thing as "pristine" Christian practice; Christians have always misappropriated the sacraments in keeping with their cultural pathologies. To use Bradshaw's language: private, public, and normative meanings often overpower and displace official intent. Nevertheless, Winner concludes her cautionary tale with a word of hope: "If they are subject to characteristic deformation and collapse upon themselves, or overflow with violence, or order the world in a distorted way; if it all will inevitably go wrong, why do we carry on with prayer and Eucharist and baptism (and silence and marriage and celibacy and song and all the other good, damaged ways we have to place ourselves somewhere where we might be found by God)? *Because they are the only things we have, and because they are gifts from the Lord.*"[12] Despite our dullness and depravity, our hope of being rescued still lies in the grace of the good Lord and in the gifts of God for the people of God. Because God offers these gifts, we can still be found.

Perhaps this confidence in being found weakens as we move from the practices of the church to the practices we find outside its walls. For although we have clear promises that God will meet us in the Word and at the Table, we have nothing quite so certain when it comes to the wider world. Yes, we know that the world belongs to God and that all people bear his image. But we are hesitant to identify the works of human culture with the work of God, especially when that work explicitly ignores God or multiplies idols to put in God's place.

There is something right about this hesitation. But one undeniable effect has been a sort of doublemindedness in which Christians are overly apprehensive about what happens outside the church and overly accommodating of what happens within. I once heard a librarian remark that

Christian colleges with strong convictions about human sin tend to have lax library security. Paradoxically, it is easier to steal books from those who believe in pervasive depravity! The librarian's point was that Christian communities often believe that they can insulate themselves from the influences of a sinful world. If there are threats, they are always on the outside, rather than within. This imaginative failure has tragically emboldened predators within the church, who take advantage of the relative absence of accountability. When it comes to cultural engagement, it has resulted in a basic posture of suspicion toward the wider culture's artifacts and resignation toward (if not outright celebration of) the mediocrity of popular "Christian" culture. Overall, it has meant that the church's encounter with culture is often characterized by reductionism, dismissiveness, and anxiety.

The burden of this book has been to sketch an alternative to this basic posture. If the preceding chapters are any indication, the interaction between theology and culture is inextricably complex, requiring humility, patience, and discernment. But we can continue the conversation, with hope. Just as with liturgical theology, the task of cultural theology is to discern what God is doing, not outside the intricacies of human making, interpretation, and judgment, but within them. For despite all the ways that we have damaged God's gifts, culture remains a place where—amid our meaning making, power struggles, work for justice, ultimate concerns, and quest for beauty—we might still be found by God. For surely principalities are not the only powers at work in creation and culture.

Interpreting Fast and Slow: Resources for Constructive Cultural Engagement

How can we move forward amid the complexity? As a start, we can live what we know, while listening to and learning from the various fields we've explored. We can't help but interpret the world, but we can become more skillful interpreters. I have been helped by thinking about cultural interpretation using what psychologists call "system 1" and "system 2," or as Daniel Kahneman puts it, "thinking fast" and "thinking slow."[13] System 1 thinking is intuitive, experiential, and effortless. Since it takes less cognitive processing, its snap judgments help us efficiently move through the world. System 2, by contrast, is deliberate, reflective, and effortful. One study found that upon meeting a new person, it takes the average American between 2.4 and 4.6 seconds to make a judgment about whether there is a potential for relationship.[14] That's system 1: "go with your gut." But impressions of others can change, and additional reflection can shift our judgments. That's system 2: "take your time."

Either system can go awry; we may jump to conclusions in system 1 or overthink things in system 2. For those who have read Jane Austen's classic novel *Pride and Prejudice*, we might say that Elizabeth Bennet is led astray by system 1 (prejudging Mr. Darcy), while Darcy is led astray by system 2 (over-rationalizing his regard for Elizabeth). But since both systems are essential for navigating the world, we need to train our intuitions and discipline our deliberations. Indeed, some psychologists, like Seymour Epstein, say that emotional intelligence reflects our ability to integrate the two systems in "constructive thinking."[15]

Perhaps *cultural* intelligence lies in a similar integration. For as we have seen, the difficulty in doing cultural interpretation is culture's complexity. Culture is multivalent: it pulls us in many directions at the same time. Unfortunately, our brains don't like ambiguity; it unsettles us, keeping us from a sense that we have a firm grip on the world. Thus, when we encounter any cultural artifact or movement, we are much more likely to use system 1. We interpret instinctively, sorting things into meaningful categories to ease the cognitive burden. In this sense, "your interpretation is your life" means that we are always already engaged in countless intuitive acts of interpretation as we navigate the world. This isn't necessarily a bad thing. But like the protagonists of Austen's story, our prejudices (and our pride!) keep us from fruitful possibilities. Growing in interpretive skill means both training our intuitions (system 1) and integrating the slower, more deliberate approach required by system 2. In a system 2 sense, "your interpretation is your life" points to the reflective integration of as many different dimensions of culture as possible.

To return to the analogy made in an earlier chapter, we can imagine ourselves moving in a field of forces, touched as it were by a thousand invisible threads of varying thickness. The threads represent both connection and direction, a "reaching out" and a "pulling in." Together these threads compose the webs of our cultural ecosystem, the strands of meaning that suspend us in our world. Some threads pull on us with great force and gravity, drawing us toward rival communities of belonging.

Five Dimensions of Cultural Interpretation

Dimension	Metaphor	Practice	Critical Mode	Questions
Meaning	Culture as immune system	Hosting	Investigative: what connects and why	How does this connect? Why do I resonate or resist?
Power	Culture as power play	Iconoclasm	Diagnostic: how power distances and directs	What are the interests of those in power? How is power's gravity exerted?
Ethical	Culture as moral boundary	Servanthood	Normative: what is good and what is right	What boundaries are provided for flourishing? How do we relate to those on the other side?
Religious	Culture as sacred experience	Discernment	Immersive: where we are anchored and pulled	What deserves attention as "sacred"? What are we doing with God?
Aesthetic	Culture as poetic project	Making	Imaginative: what could be	How does it elicit desire and delight? How does it direct desire and delight?

These represent the power dimension. Other threads have more verticality, anchoring us in the depths or drawing us up toward the heights: the threads of the religious dimension. We are often quite aware of these threads, and when they combine to give us a secure sense of what is good and right, they become the threads of the ethical dimension. Finally, there are threads that we are most actively engaged in weaving ourselves, seeking the connections that will make for the most fruitful and generative life. These represent the aesthetic dimension of culture.

Cultural interpretation always takes place within this field of forces, and we make judgments as those caught up in many meaningful threads. The theological dimension is not merely "one more thread" or one more layer to add to the others. Rather, theology is an integrative discipline; it binds together many things, while also crackling with the energy of divine action. Theology moves among the other disciplines "as one who serves" (Luke 22:27), reminding every discipline of its place before the face of God and discerning the mystery of God's work in our midst.

Theology shapes the way the conversation continues, and I want to offer three distinctive postures that accompany this constructive approach to culture. These postures follow from the theological virtues of faith, hope, and love. I will call them "non-reductive curiosity," "non-dismissive discernment," and "non-anxious presence."

Non-reductive Curiosity: The Fruit of Faith

Reductionism is the enemy of cultural interpretation because it attempts to account for all the complexity we find in creation and culture with a single mode of analysis. Perhaps this is the power lens, which wants to "follow the money" and expose the puppet masters. Or maybe it is the aesthetic lens, which is content to describe "how it moves me." As we have seen, both perspectives are valuable, but neither is sufficient in isolation. Reductionism is tempting because it simplifies, making a complex phenomenon more accessible, increasing our sense that we are in control. In the end, it craves uniformity. But since reality is like a many-sided diamond, reductionism cannot help but obscure its brilliance. In doing so it dishonors both Creator and creation.

The posture of non-reductive curiosity flows from the conviction that *faith* is irreducible to human life. This means that we are required to make claims and commitments without absolute certainty, the sort that belongs to God alone. All of us must put our whole self in, as the folk song says. Faith recognizes that we have been cast on a stage we did not make, that we are suspended in webs of meaning we have not spun, that we are vulnerable in ways we cannot escape. Reductionism attempts to escape the vulnerability of faith, seeking security in the oversimplifications of dogmatism or skepticism. As Scottish theologian Judith Wolfe puts it, "Our current academic and wider culture is either remarkably naïve or globally suspicious about this basic hermeneutical task of judgment and interpretation. It either relies overly on metrics and data—slavishly 'following the science'—or it hurries to debunk all narratives. Both are ways of eluding the responsibility of judgment and interpretation, ways of casting about for information that is unsituated, transparent, and self-interpreting."[16] Whatever information humans find, whatever meanings we make, and whatever interpretations we offer, they will always be colored by unavoidable faith commitments. This recognition removes the expectation that we can extract ourselves from our creaturely situation to gain an unambiguous, godlike view.

And yet, interpretation is our responsibility as God's creatures; we must make wise judgments as we live together in God's world. For Christians, interpretation is a practice of faith seeking understanding (Anselm's classic definition of theology). "Faith" here signifies a fundamental posture of trust, but it sets a starting point within a tradition of interpretation: we want to "go on in the same way" as those who have come before us, taking Scripture as our script. What the *Christian* faith offers is not just the admission of our creaturely vulnerability but also the invitation to rest in the embrace of the God who raised Jesus from the dead. Christian theology offers a tradition of reflection, interpretation, and devotion in response to this God, revealed in Jesus Christ through the Holy Spirit. Theology is essential because it offers us the widest possible horizon against which to set our meaning making. At its best, it is curious, desiring to learn from many voices across time and space. But at all times it listens for the voice of God, the voice of wisdom crying in the heights, the voice that we need Scripture to train us to hear.

The conviction that God speaks through the pages of Scripture requires care. We want to be biblical, but the possibility of biblicism (treating the Bible as a sort of handbook that contains *all* the answers we need) always looms as an appealing form of reductionism.[17] If we can just find a verse that tells us what to think or do, then we can get rid of some of the ambiguity that we feel. Scripture is sufficiently clear about the things that matter most; as Paul told Timothy, it is able to make us "wise for salvation through faith in Christ Jesus" (2 Tim. 3:15). But the Bible gives no clear direction on a great many cultural questions, which is why we need the system 2 deliberations of theology. Biblicism easily begets triviality (using decontextualized verses to give us "hits of meaning"); at its worst it becomes a method of justifying by proof text whatever we want to do. But to ask Scripture to be an exhaustive answer sheet is to refuse to accept what Scripture is: the theodramatic metanarrative of God's faithfulness. It is also a failure to accept the task that God has entrusted to us, that of unfolding the intricacies of creation with creativity and love. This task requires studying other things in addition to Scripture. As Calvin Seerveld writes, "When you want to find out how God ordered plants to grow, you don't go study the synoptic Gospels; you go examine plants with a sharp knife and microscope."[18] Similarly, when we want to interpret culture, discerning which creative directions are fitting for God's creational intent, we need to be able to do more than just study Scripture. We also need to bring "sharp knives and microscopes," disciplinary tools that will enable us to examine culture fruitfully and respond to culture faithfully.

This does not mean that Scripture has nothing to say about cultural discipleship. Just the opposite—to say that Scripture is our script means that it is the master narrative through which we interpret the world: creation, fall, redemption, new creation. As such, it is sufficient. We go to Scripture not to glean exhaustive information about the world but to get the right lenses for the world. The Spirit uses not individual verses but patterns of judgment—borne out across the whole of Scripture, centered in the person of Jesus Christ—to train us to order our lives to fit the story we are in. As with Holy Scripture, we trust the Holy Spirit to help us interpret the world, so that we will know what to do with the insights we find. Ultimately, our interpretation is measured by our obedience.

Non-dismissive Discernment: The Fruit of Love

But sometimes interpretation becomes an exercise in suspicion and self-satisfaction rather than love. There is another temptation we must resist: to be overly impressed with ourselves. As I mentioned above, I have made my home in a different theological tradition than the one in which I was raised. Among other reasons, I was attracted to the Dutch "Reformational" tradition because of the way it trained me to recognize the multifaceted glory of creation and the beauty of ordinary life.[19] This tradition has trained me to oppose reductionism at every turn. But the longer I have worked within it, I find that it also has some characteristic flaws: intellectualism (overreliance on analysis), triumphalism (overestimation of our ability to "transform the culture"), and parochialism (underappreciation of the gifts on the outside). I say "characteristic" flaws because these tendencies are not *essential* to the tradition—it has resources to avoid them. But they are *endemic*—widespread and commonplace. Every tradition has such flaws, and it is important that those within do our best to repair and resist their characteristic damage.

I have written this book in part because I am troubled by the dismissive tone with which many of my fellow Christians (and particularly my fellow Calvinists) approach culture. Their primary posture is suspicion, which is fine as far as it goes. But as we have seen, critiques fall flat when they are content to throw stones from outside the walls of the secular city. As Dyrness writes, "A church without an appropriate respect—even love—for its culture, will not only lack influence, but its witness will give an uncertain sound."[20]

Indeed, the tendency to assume an "omniscient narrator voice" while diagnosing cultural pathologies too often obscures the struggle that is taking place within individual hearts and within the culture at large. This struggle occurs because every person and culture lives before the face of God. We may suppress God's truth in unrighteousness (Rom. 1:18) and fail to comprehend God's light (John 1:5), but truth and light persist all the same. By the grace of God and the Spirit's power, the presence and meaning of God's attention to the world can be felt. As Jacob Klapwijk reminds us, "Self-sufficient thought, closed as it is to the truth of God, receives that truth anyway; yes, it derives its life and dynamism from its wrestling with and against that truth. . . . We must listen until we are able to hear—behind the experiences of the wrestling personality—the voice of God, who makes an appeal to the one so engaged and in and through him or her speaks to us."[21] Klapwijk argues that humility must be the foundation of any properly Christian philosophy (and I would add any Christian cultural interpretation). Humility here means an openness to God, as well as the willingness to listen to and learn from anyone willing, in good faith, to join the conversation.

Here we need fruitful models, cultural exegetes who embody practices of loving interpretation. I have been blessed to witness this through the example of a mentor, Richard Mouw, the longtime seminary president and public intellectual. In Rich I saw a way of carrying forward a theological tradition with sensitivity to its characteristic flaws. I marveled at the way that Rich held public conversations with all sorts of diverse voices like Muslims and Mormons, voices often dismissed by the broader evangelical community. Without surrendering his convictions, Rich was willing to talk to anyone, listen to anyone, learn from anyone. He was a model of careful discernment, always in search of clarity—but discernment meant taking his conversation partners incredibly seriously. This was non-dismissive discernment at its best—theology *for* culture—a model that I am endeavoring to follow in my own work.[22]

The great temptation in polarizing times is not only to dismiss the opinions of those with whom we disagree but also to avoid their company. Such a dismissal refuses the challenge of their presence, finds reasons to discount their contributions, even reinscribes the division between clean and unclean (discussed in chap. 1). But just as love flows from faith, the refusal to reduce cultural artifacts entails the refusal to dismiss culture makers, even if we feel visceral resistance to their cultural work. It must have felt so difficult for the Jewish brothers and sisters to join gentiles— those "repugnant cultural others"[23]—at the table in those early days. But it was what the gospel required (Gal. 2). As a gentile, I am thankful.

Non-dismissive discernment recognizes the dignity of all of God's creatures, especially those who bear God's image. Even more, it begins by recognizing the most vulnerable among us, whose personhood and belonging have been called into question as a matter of course.[24] Even if we disagree with the conclusions of our conversation partners, we must refuse to dismiss their dignity. This will mean relationships marked by creative tension, in which gaps in understanding or agreement are crossed by the practices of empathy and love. There may be occasions for breaking fellowship, but it is always an extreme measure. In all things, we must remember the example of our Lord, who "welcomes sinners and eats with them" (Luke 15:2). We are the sinners.

Non-anxious Presence: The Fruit of Hope

Perhaps what is most needed in an anxious age is simply the capacity to be present, to be what Rabbi Edwin Friedman calls a "non-anxious presence." Poorly differentiated individuals, Friedman argues, take on the anxiety of others, becoming quickly overwhelmed by the weight of it all. Friedman finds that effective service is a matter of self-differentiation, the ability to remain connected to others without absorbing their anxiety, whether in the form of anger, fear, cynicism, or despair.[25] This does not mean rejecting empathy, embracing stoicism, or trying to fly above the fray. Rather, it means having a clear sense of your limitations and callings, learning to be present without needing to control the response of others.

Not long ago I was invited by an online acquaintance to join him for his denomination's local meeting. I'm not sure why I agreed. The older I get, the more I gravitate to spaces in which I am comfortable, where I know what will be asked of me, spaces where I have some measure of power, influence, and control. Perhaps this is true of most of us, even if the privilege to choose the spaces where we work is not shared by all. Members of minority communities are often quite adept at moving in majority spaces, and it is valuable for members of majority communities more regularly to feel the vulnerability of the outsider. But it occurred to me as I felt all the awkwardness of being a stranger at this particular meeting that remaining in such a space required me to grow in resilience. There is risk in sitting at someone else's table, wondering whether and how you will be welcomed. Being a guest was good for me; it reminded me what it is like to enter a place where I have little recognition and to learn to be present in a way characterized by openness rather than anxiety.

Perhaps this kind of non-anxious joining is the form of hospitality that we see most visibly in the ministry of Jesus, who set few tables of his own. Instead, he joined others, accepting their invitations, sharing their food, suffering their judgment. Jesus was never governed by reactive anxiety; his mission was clarified and guided by the Father's love. At one of the parties that Jesus attended, the bride and the groom ran out of wine for their guests. This led his mother, Mary, to involve her son: "They have no more wine." Jesus's reply is startling: "Why do you involve me? . . . My hour has not yet come" (John 2:3–4). Whatever Mary's intent in asking the question, Jesus challenged her expectations. New Testament scholar D. A. Carson writes that Jesus is declaring "his utter freedom from any kind of human advice, agenda, or manipulation. He has embarked on his ministry, the purpose of his coming; his only guiding star is his heavenly Father's will."[26] The freedom of Jesus to be present without justification was rooted in the Father's pleasure ("This is my son" [Matt. 3:17]), rather than in the short-sighted judgments of his community or culture ("He saved others; himself he cannot save" [Matt. 27:42 KJV]). The power to be present, free from the need to control or be controlled by the actions of others, is only possible if our hope is rooted in the same soil, the humble confidence of the Father's love. If this is true—that we are held in the love of our good Lord—then we need not fear even the most hostile cultural settings (Luke 21:16–18).

It is not incidental that John tells us when the wineless wedding occurred: "On the third day a wedding took place" (John 2:1). The literary clue foreshadows something even more joyous and unprecedented that would happen at the dawn of another third day when, against all expectation, Jesus would take death and overthrow it. His action would be different from what any of the disciples expected. But it was better than any of them could dream.

When it comes to our cultural work, we may have many expectations for how God might use our efforts. It may be impossible not to have expectations. But it is possible to hold our expectations loosely, without ultimate anxiety. It is enough to know that God is present, and so to offer our work up with joy, even allowing it to die, to fail, to be forgotten. Who knows? Maybe it will be resurrected and filled full in the age to come.

While we wait for the kingdom to arrive, we can take our small boats out onto the ocean of meaning. As one of my favorite confessions reminds me, the universe is "like a beautiful book in which all creatures great and small are as letters to make us ponder the invisible things of God."[27] There is *so much meaning*. And we, too, get to add some letters and lines to the story. Like the Corinthian believers, we are "living letters," known and read by everyone (2 Cor. 3:2). May our words and works be in tune (Ps. 19:14)!

But it should give us great comfort to know that God alone gives the definitive interpretation, the final translation of all our work. As John Donne reminds us, "All mankind is of one author, and is one volume; when one man dies, one chapter is not torn out of the book, but translated into a better language; and every chapter must be so translated; God employs several translators; some pieces are translated by age, some by sickness, some by war, some by justice; but God's hand is in every translation, and his hand shall bind up all our scattered leaves again, for that library where every book shall lie open to one another."[28] We cannot avoid interpreting our world, and we cannot avoid the interpretation that is our life. But we can hope that God will take up our life's work and make it matter in ways we cannot foresee.

For the ultimate significance of all our culture making rests not in human hands but in the long and loving work of God, who gathers up "our scattered leaves" into a better book, translated into a better language, with words that will resound forever—let all creation sing!

QUESTIONS FOR
REFLECTION AND DISCUSSION

1. What has been your experience with the practice of Communion? How does changing the manner or frequency of the practice affect the meaning? How could this case study be applied to other church and cultural practices?

2. How could liturgical theology's categories of official meaning, private meaning, public meaning, and normative meaning give us greater nuance in the way we describe cultural artifacts and practices? Is there another example that you could describe in terms of these layers of meaning?

3. Cultural intelligence may be found in the integration of "interpreting fast" and "interpreting slow"—our intuition (system 1) and our analysis (system 2). What are the benefits and drawbacks of each form of interpretation, and what would it mean to integrate them?

4. Of the three postures outlined in this chapter—non-reductive curiosity, non-dismissive discernment, and non-anxious presence—which is the most difficult to cultivate? What are the forces that work against them, and how can we develop them more fruitfully?

5. Having completed this book, what would you now say is the meaning of the phrase "your interpretation is your life"?

APPENDIX

Looking through the Lenses—
Questions to Ask about Cultural Artifacts

One of the best ways we can begin to navigate the complexity of culture is by asking the right questions. To ask a question about a cultural artifact is to pull on a particular thread of meaning; together, these questions help us give thicker descriptions of what is going on.

In courses I teach on theology and culture, I ask students to offer Christian interpretations of various cultural artifacts and trends. The results are always enjoyable to read, concerned with fascinating topics: contemporary nostalgia, sympathy for villains, mindfulness, minimalism, the tiny-house movement, as well as numerous examples from the world of entertainment. I have learned much from these essays and have been inspired by my students' thoughtfulness and verve.

To make the method more accessible, I encourage them to think in two movements (described in the introduction): first, theology *from* culture, and second, theology *for* culture.

1. Theology from *culture: What is a "thick description" of this cultural artifact?* Theology from culture is an exercise in listening and learning from the cultural artifact or trend. The questions we ask in this mode are investigative and empathetic as we seek to understand its implicit theology or imaginative vision. I want students to demonstrate that they have wrestled with the complexity and are able to articulate why this cultural phenomenon has connected with so many people.

2. *Theology* for *culture: What should be our "lived interpretation" of this cultural artifact?* Theology for culture is an exercise in discerning and directing our cultural discipleship. The questions we ask in this mode are critical and constructive as we seek to live out distinctively Christian interpretations of culture's offerings. I want students to tell me how the gospel of Jesus critiques and completes the world of meaning found in cultural artifacts.

Within this general framework (listen, then speak), I also offer students the following questions for getting at each of the five dimensions this book explores. In general, the questions for each dimension follow the same logic, moving from investigation to evaluation. Given the particular cultural artifact under investigation, some questions may be more relevant than others. The goal is not to answer all the questions but rather to address the cultural artifact from multiple angles with a long and loving look.

The Meaning Dimension: Culture as Immune System

1. Is this "a thing"? In other words, does this cultural artifact represent something shared by many people rather than being peculiar to a few people? Why is this "a thing"? Why has it "gone viral"?

2. How does this thing connect? Why do people find this meaningful?

3. Why do I resonate or resist this thing? What does it mean to me, and why?

4. How does it connect with Christian accounts of the world? Does it emerge from within or outside Christian cultures? How have Christians embraced or resisted this thing?

5. Where do we see glimmers of beauty, goodness, and truth?

6. How does this cultural artifact fit into and express the movements of the biblical story (created goodness, pervasive fallenness, or hope of redemption)?

The Power Dimension: Culture as Power Play

1. What are the interests of those in power when it comes to this cultural artifact?

2. Who benefits from the success of this cultural artifact? Who does not benefit? Who does it place in the center? Who does it push to the margins?

3. How could this artifact be used to exercise influence, constrain desire, serve as propaganda, or support the status quo?

4. Should/can we resist? What makes resistance difficult?

5. Where do we see cultural idolatry—a good thing that has been made into an ultimate thing? Is there a connection to be made between the cultural idolatry and occasions of cultural injustice?

6. What would iconoclasm (confronting idolatry) look like? What, if anything, needs to be rejected or replaced? What needs to be complicated? What critique does the gospel bring?

The Ethical Dimension: Culture as Moral Boundary

1. What boundaries are provided by the people who participate in this cultural phenomenon? What is deemed acceptable, normal, desirable, or virtuous behavior?

2. What is the implicit vision of human flourishing (what it means to be a good human) according to this cultural artifact? Where is the moral high ground?

3. How does this artifact's vision of flourishing fit the Christian vision of righteousness, peace, and joy?

4. How does this cultural artifact lead us to relate to those on the other side of the moral boundary, and how does this compare with how Scripture leads us?

5. What do we make of this artifact if we are ultimately answerable to God?

6. How can we participate in this cultural phenomenon in a way that leads to the organic flourishing of others?

The Religious Dimension: Culture as Sacred Experience

1. When it comes to this cultural artifact, what deserves attention as "sacred"? What is worthy of our ultimate concern?

2. How does this cultural artifact help people cope with the difficulties of life? How does it organize life into a consistent rhythm, even ritual behavior?

3. How does this cultural phenomenon form a community of support, and what are the common things in the center?

4. How might it offer transcendence of self-interest, even moments of ecstasy?

5. What are those who participate in this cultural phenomenon doing with God? Is it a way to avoid God? Where are there "cracks" to let God's light in?

6. What challenge, critique, or completion does the gospel bring to the religious vision of this cultural artifact? How does the gospel offer fuller meaning that could not be found apart from Christ?

The Aesthetic Dimension: Culture as Poetic Project

1. How does this cultural artifact elicit desire and delight?

2. What is the implicit vision of the beautiful and worthwhile life?

3. How do appearances play into the felt experience of the cultural trend? What are the "branding" elements that associate this cultural artifact with what is desirable?

4. How is this cultural artifact generative, and what does it generate? What are some ways that participants have taken this in surprising ways? Does it include a layer of excess, "just for the heaven of it"?

5. How does Christian faith direct the desire and delight this cultural artifact elicits? What are we being trained to love, and how can the love of God reorient these desires?

6. What will I make of this cultural phenomenon? How will this be integrated into my life? What will I make in response to this cultural phenomenon?

NOTES

Introduction   Is There Anything to Say?

1. Smith with Denton, *Soul Searching*, 133. Smith and Denton's name for this theology—"moralistic therapeutic deism"—sought to identify the working theology of a generation. Among Christian ministers, writers, and academics, it was the diagnosis that launched a thousand doctors, searching for the cure for such defective discipleship and calling for a renewed commitment to catechesis. My class prompt, "What do you believe, and what difference does it make in your life?" is inspired by Smith and Denton's study.

2. Swinburne, "Garden of Proserpine."

3. Portions of this section were originally published as a short think piece for an online journal and are reproduced here with permission. See J. A. Bailey, "Shows That Shape Us."

4. Marshall McLuhan is famous for his argument that "societies have always been shaped more by the nature of media by which men communicate than by the content of the communication." McLuhan and Fiore, *Medium Is the Massage*, 8.

5. For an account of the biblical theme of wisdom in relationship to a theology of culture, see Dyrness, *Facts on the Ground*.

6. See, for example, Lyden and Mazur, *Routledge Companion to Religion*.

7. See, for example, Terry Muck's definition: "The modern, scholarly study of religion is the comprehensive study of religion and religions as human phenomena using both historical and systematic methodologies, as far as possible without dogmatic presuppositions, comparing and contrasting both universal and particular features of those religions." Muck, *Why Study Religion?*, 22.

8. Forbes and Mahan, *Religion and Popular Culture*, 9.

9. Walls, *Missionary Movement in Christian History*, 6–9.

10. By "global Christianity" I mean the traditions of scriptural interpretation throughout church history as well as across geographical space. See the excellent discussion in Billings, *Word of God*.

11. Marsh and Ortiz, *Explorations in Theology and Film*, 24.

12. Edgar, *Created and Creating*, 174.

13. For a fuller version of this critique, see Tanner, *Theories of Culture*.

14. As Abraham Kuyper put it, "We must, in every domain, discover the treasures and develop the potencies hidden by God in nature and in human life." Kuyper, *Lectures on Calvinism*, 31.

15. Dyrness, *Poetic Theology*, 38.

16. I learned this phrase from Richard Mouw, who expounds this theme in Kuyper. See, for example, Mouw, *Abraham Kuyper*, 15–18.

17. See this distinction in Richter, *Epic of Eden*, 21–23.

18. Fujimura, *Art and Faith*, 72.

19. This section is deeply marked by the vision set out by my teacher Kevin J. Vanhoozer in several of his books, most notably in *Drama of Doctrine*.

20. Vanhoozer, "What Is Everyday Theology?" in Vanhoozer, Anderson, and Sleasman, *Everyday Theology*, 56. The artifacts examined in these chapters testify to the problem with books on popular culture: most are quite dated if not passé. (I am thinking here primarily of my own essay about the now-defunct site Xanga!)

21. Dyrness, *Poetic Theology*, 73.

22. See my analysis in J. A. Bailey, "Theodramatic Imagination," 455–70.

Chapter 1 The Meaning Dimension

1. Cronk, *That Complex Whole*, 87.

2. I am thankful to my colleague Jeff Ploegstra for teaching me about viruses and helping me make the biological analogy in this chapter.

3. For this reason, Callaway and Batali prefer to speak of cultural "traces" rather than cultural "texts." Traces leave something with us. Callaway and Batali, *Watching TV Religiously*, 8–9.

4. The danger—as in some evolutionary accounts—is reductionism. But it should be possible to give an account of culture that is rooted in the physical world without reducing the riches of culture to a mechanism for preserving our genes. For an antidote to this reductionism, see Robinson, *Absence of Mind*.

5. Donald, *Mind So Rare*, 298.

6. Dawkins, *Selfish Gene*.

7. Geertz, *Interpretation of Cultures*, 152.

8. I am indebted to Justin Wells for helping me frame things this way.

9. Haidt, *Righteous Mind*, 85.

10. Sloterdijk, *Bubbles*, 25.

11. Sloterdijk's story is what Canadian philosopher Charles Taylor calls a "subtraction story," in which the transcendent is removed because it is no longer necessary. By contrast, Taylor argues that we have constructed an insulating, immanent frame to shut out the transcendent. See Taylor, *Secular Age*.

12. Skillen, *God's Sabbath with Creation*, 51.

13. Richter, *Epic of Eden*, 111.

14. Aronofsky, *Noah*.

15. H. Bavinck, "Common Grace," 51.

16. Lewis, *Mere Christianity*, 50.

17. Morales suggests that the garden, the region of Eden, and the land east of Eden (where Cain settles) correspond to the Holy of Holies, Holy Place, and Outer Court of the Tabernacle, as humanity moves further and further from the presence of God, leading to the reversal of the cosmos back into chaos through the waters of the flood. Morales, *Who Shall Ascend*, 65.

18. Morales, *Who Shall Ascend*, 161.

19. Hauerwas, "Abortion," in *Hauerwas Reader*, 609.

20. Haidt, *Righteous Mind*, 179.

21. See Eglinton, "Let Every Tongue Confess," 35–46.

22. Lewis, *Mere Christianity*, 175–77.

23. We can add one more set of metaphors from Herman Bavinck, who discussed the gospel as both pearl and leaven. As a pearl of infinite value, the gospel is a treasure in itself, independent of any culture influence it might have (Matt. 13:45–46). As a leaven, the germ of the gospel permeates society with "culture making, culture swaying, and culture transforming power." See the discussion in Driesenga, "Pearl and a Leaven," 42.

24. See this argument developed in Edgar, *Created and Creating.*

25. J. H. Bavinck, *Introduction to the Science of Missions,* 178–79.

26. Pohl, *Making Room.*

Chapter 2   The Power Dimension

1. Godwin, "Meme, Counter-Meme."

2. See the discussion in Boersma, *Violence, Hospitality, and the Cross,* 31.

3. See Noll, *Civil War as a Theological Crisis.*

4. Parker, Minkin, and Bennett, "Economic Fallout from COVID-19."

5. Clouser, *Myth of Religious Neutrality.*

6. Marx, "Theses on Feuerbach," in *Selected Writings,* 101 (emphasis original).

7. For one account of this long shadow, see Taylor, *Sources of the Self.*

8. Stazler, *Parks and Recreation,* 2011, season 3, episode 2, "Flu Season."

9. See these critiques and rejoinders in Eagleton, *Why Marx Was Right.*

10. Marx and Engels, *Communist Manifesto,* 13.

11. Eagleton, *Why Marx Was Right,* 34. We should pause to distinguish between Marxist analysis and Marxism: the former seeks to bring an economic critique; the latter weds itself to other grand theories to become a "theory of everything." It is possible for a person to find Marxism and Christianity to be diametrically opposed (Marxism as grand theory), while it is also possible for a person to identify as a Marxist Christian (using Marxist economic analysis).

12. "[It is] a religion in the sense that it too is a faith . . . [and] because it has substituted for the consciousness of the transcendental God of the Catholics, trust in man and his best strengths as the sole spiritual reality." Gramsci, "Audacia e Fede," quoted in R. Smith, "Cultural Marxism," 444.

13. Gutiérrez, *Theology of Liberation.*

14. See Horkheimer, "Traditional and Critical Theory," in *Critical Theory,* 188–243.

15. See the discussion in Cobb, *Blackwell Guide to Theology,* 45–51.

16. See the summary in R. Smith, "Cultural Marxism," 463.

17. Langberg, *Redeeming Power,* 190.

18. Here I am concerned with the academic discipline of critical race theory and the more popular anti-racism movement, which is adjacent but distinct. For an introduction to the former, see Delgado and Stefancic, *Critical Race Theory.*

19. R. Smith, "Cultural Marxism," 461–62.

20. Derrick Bell, the creator of CRT, asserts that his work is shaped by Black voices rather than European ones ("I think there must be value in Marxist and other writings, but I did not really read them in college and have had little time since"). Curry, "Saved by the Bell," 44.

21. See, for example, Bowens, *African American Readings of Paul.*

22. This is the critical question, as Nicholas Wolterstorff asks: "What can be done to get people to acknowledge the dignity of their fellow human beings, to recognize when their dignity is being violated, and to act accordingly?" Wolterstorff, *Journey toward Justice,* 165.

23. King himself draws this description from Archbishop William Temple. See King, *Strength to Love,* 98–100.

24. Smedes, *My God and I*, 59.

25. McCaulley, "I Have Only One Hope."

26. Rookmaaker, *Creative Gift*, 58.

27. Charles and Rah, *Unsettling Truths*.

28. Barr, "Symbolism of Names."

29. See the discussion in Foucault, *Foucault Reader*, 8–11.

30. See Rothstein, *Color of Law*.

31. "Name," in Ryken, Wilhoit, and Longman, *Dictionary of Biblical Imagery*, 583.

32. Tisby, *How to Fight Racism*, 1n (emphasis original).

33. Jennings, *Christian Imagination*, 7–8.

34. Theologian Natalie Carnes notes, "These image fighters did not come with hammers but with laws; they did not physically destroy an image but circumscribed its appearance in the world." Carnes, *Image and Presence*, 2.

35. Carnes, "Breaking the Power of Monuments."

36. Calvin, *Institutes* 1.11.8

37. See the discussion in Crouch, *Playing God*, 10–12, 54–84.

38. Koyzis, *Political Visions and Illusions*.

39. Carnes, *Image and Presence*, 157–58. Carnes shows that we find both kinds of iconoclasm in Jesus's own account of the Last Judgment in Matt. 25: "You think you are sheep, but really you are goats" (cancellation). "You thought you were doing unto the least of these but also you were doing unto me" (complication). See Carnes, *Image and Presence*, 158.

40. Adichie, "Danger of a Single Story."

41. Brueggemann, *Prophetic Imagination*, 99.

Chapter 3 The Ethical Dimension

1. One tragic story among many is the death of Sandra Bland, memorably recounted in Gladwell, *Talking to Strangers*.

2. This is Cornelius Plantinga Jr.'s description of sin. Plantinga, *Not the Way It's Supposed to Be*.

3. Chesterton, "Our Note Book," 780.

4. This "pervasive interpretive pluralism" has often been blamed on the Protestant Reformation, but it seems to me that it is simply a feature of the human condition. See the use of this phrase in C. Smith, *Bible Made Impossible*.

5. Grenz and Franke, *Beyond Foundationalism*, 166.

6. Wolterstorff, *Justice*, 145.

7. Sandel, *Justice*.

8. Rawls, *Theory of Justice*.

9. MacIntyre, *After Virtue*, 216.

10. Haidt, *Righteous Mind*, 146.

11. Haidt, *Righteous Mind*, 178–79.

12. Haidt, *Righteous Mind*, 214.

13. Zahl, *Seculosity*, xii.

14. Crouch, "Return of Shame."

15. Plato, *Republic of Plato*, 37–38.

16. A. Plantinga, *Where the Conflict Really Lies*.

17. Barrett, *Born Believers*.

18. See this argument in Taylor, *Secular Age*.

19. Luhrmann, *How God Becomes Real*, 154.

20. Lewis, *Mere Christianity*, 74.

21. See this argument in Jennings, *Christian Imagination*, chap. 1.

22. The concept of answerability draws from a literary tradition: answerability is a matter of responsiveness to the world around us and our accountability for what we say and do. See Bakhtin, *Art and Answerability*.

23. Vanhoozer, *Remythologizing Theology*, 319.

24. Crouch, *Playing God*, 68.

25. Vanhoozer, *Remythologizing Theology*, 319.

26. Niebuhr, *Christ and Culture*.

27. Quoted in Coles, *Call of Service*, 32. Coles is transcribing his own recording of a midday address by Dr. King at the Southern Regional Council in the spring of 1964.

28. Volf, *Exclusion and Embrace*, 125.

29. H. Bavinck, *Reformed Ethics*, 39.

30. Crouch, *Playing God*, 10.

31. Koyzis, *We Answer to Another*, 78–81.

32. I am thankful to Dordt University's dean of chapel, Aaron Baart, for making this connection quite brilliantly in a chapel message in response to Dias, "'Christianity Will Have Power.'" Aaron Baart, "Get Set," Chapel message, Sioux Center, IA. September 10, 2020.

33. J. H. Bavinck, *Impact of Christianity*, 132, quoted in Visser, *Heart for the Gospel*, 259–60.

34. As Gandalf and the Fellowship set themselves against the powers of evil, Gandalf says, "But, for all their cunning, we have one advantage. The Ring remains hidden. And that we should seek to destroy it has not yet entered their darkest dreams." Tolkien, *Two Towers*, 100.

35. Tolkien, *Return of the King*, 30. Alan Jacobs makes this connection even more eloquently in his discussion of what he calls the "The Gandalf Option." Jacobs, "Plurality and Unity."

36. Volf and McAnnally-Linz, *Public Faith in Action*, 15.

37. Wolterstorff, *Journey toward Justice*, 242.

38. Gramsci, *Selections from the Prison Notebooks*, 5–23. See a similar use of this concept in Vanhoozer, Anderson, and Sleasman, *Everyday Theology*, 57.

39. Smedes, *My God and I*, 59.

Chapter 4   The Religious Dimension

1. Red Carpet News TV, "Bill Murray Admits."

2. See, for example, Loconte, *Hobbit, a Wardrobe, and a Great War*.

3. Tolkien, *Letters*, 262.

4. "Immortality projects" is Sam Keen's summary, from the foreword of Becker, *Denial of Death*, xiii.

5. Ingmar Bergman, *The Seventh Seal*.

6. Wilfred Cantwell Smith's suggestion that religion works better as an adjective ("religious") than as a noun is worth following. W. Smith, *Meaning and End of Religion*, 20–22.

7. E. Bailey, "Implicit Religion," 271–78.

8. Parsons, *Being Spiritual but Not Religious*.

9. J. E. Smith, *Religious but Not Religious*.

10. Ter Kuile and Thurston, "How We Gather."

11. Burton, *Strange Rites*, 10–11.

12. Burton, *Strange Rites*, 13.

13. Haidt, *Righteous Mind*, 264.

14. Durkheim, *Elementary Forms of Religious Life*, 217.

15. Berger, *Sacred Canopy*.

16. Abraham Kuyper argues that, against this universal phenomenon, the Protestant recovery of the doctrine of the "priesthood of all believers" is a great gift to the world. Kuyper, *Lectures on Calvinism*, 47.

17. Žižek, "If There Is a God."

18. See this point in Wallace, *This Is Water*.

19. This is a turn of Haidt's phrase "morality binds and blinds." Haidt, *Righteous Mind*, 369.

20. Schleiermacher, *On Religion*.

21. Otto, *Idea of the Holy*, 12.

22. Grahame, *Annotated Wind in the Willows*, 176–77.

23. Otto, *Idea of the Holy*, 55.

24. Tillich, *Theology of Culture*, 9.

25. Tracy, *Blessed Rage for Order*, 53.

26. Tracy, *Blessed Rage for Order*, 105.

27. Tracy, *Analogical Imagination*, 108.

28. Tracy, *Analogical Imagination*, 163.

29. Lindbeck, *Nature of Doctrine*.

30. Bonhoeffer, *Letters and Papers*, 312.

31. Esack, *On Being a Muslim*, 25, 37.

32. For a fuller account, see Netland, *Encountering Religious Pluralism*.

33. Lewis, *Mere Christianity*, 29.

34. J. H. Bavinck, *Introduction to the Science of Missions*, 237.

35. See the discussion in Johnston, *God's Wider Presence*, 114–16.

36. Barth, *On Religion*, 72.

37. On translating *Aufhebung* (which Barth borrows from Hegel) as "sublimation" rather than "abolition," see Green's introduction in Barth, *On Religion*, 5–7.

38. Barth, *On Religion*, 111.

39. Elizondo, *Galilean Journey*, 103.

40. See the excellent discussion in Barfield, *Ancient Quarrel*, 79.

41. J. H. Bavinck, *Church between Temple and Mosque*, 18.

42. J. H. Bavinck, *Introduction to the Science of Missions*, 242–44.

43. Mandelbaum's translation of the last line of Dante, *Paradiso* 33:145. See Alighieri, *Divine Comedy*.

Chapter 5 The Aesthetic Dimension

1. Lasseter, *Toy Story*.

2. Edelstein, Willmore, Ebiri, and Bastién, "Every Movie of the 2010s, Ranked."

3. Eliot, *Notes towards the Definition of Culture*, 26.

4. It is for this reason that Calvin Seerveld argues for "allusiveness" as the norm of aesthetics. Seerveld, *Rainbows for the Fallen World*, 126–35.

5. Brown, *Religious Aesthetics*, 22.

6. Dyrness, *Facts on the Ground*, 34.

7. See, for example, de Botton, *Religion for Atheists*, 207–46.

8. Dubin, *Rodgers & Hammerstein's Cinderella*.

9. Plato, *Dialogues of Plato*, 154–56.

10. Lovejoy, *Great Chain of Being*.

11. See this quote and the discussion in Tatarkiewicz, "Great Theory of Beauty," 170.

12. Milbank, Ward, and Wyschogrod, *Theological Perspectives on God and Beauty*, 3.

13. Hume, *Standard of Taste*, 7.

14. This line comes from the Coen brothers' inimitable movie *The Big Lebowski*.

15. Hume, *Standard of Taste*, 17–18.

16. Dutton, *Art Instinct*, 19–23.

17. Dutton, "Darwinian Theory of Beauty."

18. Noted in Martel, *Reclaiming Art*.

19. Rilke, "Archaic Torso of Apollo."

20. Martel, *Reclaiming Art*, xv.

21. Martel, *Reclaiming Art*, 26–27. My thanks to Justin Wells for helping me clarify my thinking in this section, and for recommending Martel's book.

22. See this argument in Fujimura, *Art and Faith*, 15.

23. Pieper, *Leisure*.

24. Wolterstorff, *In This World of Wonders*, 260.

25. As Dutch anthropologist Johan Huizinga wrote in his groundbreaking study, play is always "accompanied by a feeling of tension, joy, and consciousness that is different from ordinary life." Huizinga, *Homo Ludens*, 28.

26. Dyrness, *Poetic Theology*, 271.

27. Dyrness goes on, "Since symbolic practices are fundamental to human flourishing, any project of human betterment will seek to appreciate and celebrate the aesthetic impulse that is already present in the community." Dyrness, *Poetic Theology*, 254.

28. So also with the "words of the wise" (Prov. 22:17–24:22, adapted from the Egyptian Instruction of Amenemope) and the words of King Lemuel (Prov. 31). See the discussion in Johnston, *God's Wider Presence*, 77.

29. Brueggemann, "Shape for Old Testament Theology, II," 395–415.

30. See my own attempt in J. A. Bailey, *Reimagining Apologetics*.

31. See this phrase, which the authors draw from René Girard, in Goudzwaard and Bartholomew, *Beyond the Modern Age*, 165.

32. Lewis, *Screwtape Letters*, 44.

33. Coakley, *God, Sexuality and the Self*, 6, 10.

34. Lewis, *Silver Chair*, 23.

35. Coakley, *God, Sexuality and the Self*, 16.

36. Seerveld, *Rainbows for the Fallen World*, 13.

37. I first heard this wonderful phrase in a personal conversation with Robert Johnston.

38. Robinson, *What Are We Doing Here?*, 33.

39. Lee, "From Blossoms," 54. My thanks to Rylan Brue for helping me make this connection.

40. Lewis, *Weight of Glory*, 41.

41. See, for example, Kuyper, *Lectures on Calvinism*, 155.

42. D. Steven Long, "Eschatology, Apocalyptic, Ethics, and Political Theology," in Green, Pardue, and Yeo, *Majority World Theology*, 610–11.

43. Tolkien, *Tree and Leaf*, 60.

44. Tolkien, *Tree and Leaf*, 68–69 (emphasis added).

45. MacDonald, *Dish of Orts*, 12.

46. Robinson, *Housekeeping*, 92.

47. Hyde, *Gift*, xvi–xvii. My thanks to Makoto Fujimura for recommending this book to me, and for his influence on this chapter.

Conclusion The Lived Dimension

1. It is for this reason, the focus on human agency, that Dyrness finds "cultural wisdom" to be a more fruitful category than "common grace" when it comes to discussing God's work outside the walls of the church. Dyrness, *Facts on the Ground*, 26–31.

2. As George MacDonald puts it, "Your theory is not your faith. . . . Your faith is your obedience." MacDonald, *Unspoken Sermons*, 532.

3. This has been called "the turn to practice." In contrast to approaches that focus on beliefs or experience, theologians like George Lindbeck emphasize the way that Christian practices provide a grammar within which Christian faith becomes meaningful. Lindbeck, *Nature of Doctrine*.

4. J. K. A. Smith, *You Are What You Love*, 27.

5. J. K. A. Smith, *Desiring the Kingdom*, 40.

6. Bradshaw, "Difficulties," 181.

7. See this phrase in Lathrop, *Holy Things*, 80–81.

8. Bradshaw, "Difficulties," 189. Bradshaw further divides the *official* meaning into the meaning intended by the original compilers of a rite and the meaning attached by subsequent generations. Indeed, it is difficult to adjudicate whose meaning gets to be the official one! My thanks to Cory Willson for directing me to Hoffman through Bradshaw.

9. Bradshaw, "Difficulties," 191. In liturgical terms, the relationship of *lex orandi* and *lex credendi* is reciprocal.

10. I am thankful to my colleague David Westfall for pointing this out to me (many times).

11. J. K. A. Smith, *Desiring the Kingdom*, 93–104.

12. Winner, *Dangers of Christian Practice*, 137 (emphasis added).

13. Kahneman, *Thinking, Fast and Slow*.

14. See Elmer, *Cross-Cultural Servanthood*, 48.

15. Epstein, *Constructive Thinking*.

16. Wolfe, "Relevance of Theology."

17. I am interacting with biblicism as defined in C. Smith, *Bible Made Impossible*.

18. Seerveld, *Rainbows for the Fallen World*, 13.

19. This tradition is represented by theologians like Abraham Kuyper and Herman Bavinck and by philosopher Herman Dooyeweerd. See Bartholomew, *Contours of the Kuyperian Tradition*.

20. Dyrness, *Facts on the Ground*, 22.

21. Klapwijk, "Antithesis and Common Grace," 140.

22. Mouw, *Uncommon Decency*.

23. Harding, "Representing Fundamentalism," 373–93. See the discussion in Jacobs, *How to Think*, 26–27.

24. In Catholic social teaching, this is commonly known as the "preferential option for the poor." See United States Conference of Catholic Bishops, "Option for the Poor and Vulnerable."

25. Friedman, *Failure of Nerve*. I am adopting Friedman's term without necessarily endorsing the sweeping proposals for "non-anxious" leadership, which in my opinion underestimates the importance of empathy. Friedman's theory may thus be leveraged in service of narcissistic leadership, against Friedman's intent, which seeks organic integrity rather than autocracy. In my understanding, non-anxious presence is always accompanied by non-dismissive discernment.

26. Carson, *Gospel according to John*, 171.

27. De Brès, "Belgic Confession," 26.

28. Donne, *Devotions upon Emergent Occasions*, 102.

BIBLIOGRAPHY

Adichie, Chimamanda Ngozi. "The Danger of a Single Story." TED. You-Tube video, 19:33. October 7, 2009. https://www.youtube.com/watch?v=D9Ihs241zeg.

Alighieri, Dante. *The Divine Comedy: Inferno; Purgatorio; Paradiso*. Translated by Allen Mandelbaum. New York: Everyman's Library, 1995.

Aronofsky, Darren, dir. *Noah*. United States: Paramount Pictures, 2014.

Bailey, Edward. "Implicit Religion." *Religion* 40, no. 4 (2010): 271–78.

Bailey, Justin Ariel. *Reimagining Apologetics: The Beauty of Faith in a Secular Age*. Downers Grove, IL: IVP Academic, 2020.

———. "Shows That Shape Us: Asking the Right Questions." *In All Things*, January 21, 2020. https://inallthings.org/shows-that-shape-us-asking-the-right-questions/.

———. "The Theodramatic Imagination: Spirit and Imagination in the Work of Kevin Vanhoozer." *International Journal of Public Theology* 12 (2018): 455–70.

Bakhtin, M. M. *Art and Answerability: Early Philosophical Essays*. Edited by Michael Holquist. Translated by Vadim Liapunov. Austin: University of Texas Press, 1990.

Barfield, Raymond. *The Ancient Quarrel between Philosophy and Poetry*. Cambridge: Cambridge University Press, 2011.

Barr, James. "The Symbolism of Names in the Old Testament." *Bulletin of John Rylands Library* 52, no. 1 (February 1969): 11–29.

Barrett, Justin L. *Born Believers: The Science of Children's Religious Belief.* New York: Atria Books, 2012.

Barth, Karl. *On Religion: The Revelation of God as the Sublimation of Religion.* Translated by Garrett Green. New York: T&T Clark, 2007.

Bartholomew, Craig G. *Contours of the Kuyperian Tradition: A Systematic Introduction.* Downers Grove, IL: IVP Academic, 2021.

Bavinck, Herman. "Common Grace." *Calvin Theological Journal* 24, no. 1 (1989): 35–65.

———. *Reformed Ethics: Created, Fallen, and Converted Humanity.* Edited by John Bolt. Translated by Jessica Joustra, Nelson Kloosterman, Antoine Theron, and Dirk van Keulen. Grand Rapids: Baker Academic, 2019.

Bavinck, Johan Herman. *The Church between Temple and Mosque: A Study of the Relationship between the Christian Faith and Other Religions.* Grand Rapids: Eerdmans, 1981.

———. *The Impact of Christianity on the Non-Christian World.* Grand Rapids: Eerdmans, 1949.

———. *An Introduction to the Science of Missions.* Translated by David Hugh Freeman. Phillipsburg, NJ: Presbyterian and Reformed, 1960.

Becker, Ernest. *The Denial of Death.* New York: Simon & Schuster, 2007.

Berger, Peter L. *The Sacred Canopy: Elements of a Sociological Theory of Religion.* Garden City, NY: Doubleday, 1967.

Bergman, Ingmar, dir. *The Seventh Seal.* Irvington, NY: Criterion Collection, 1998.

Billings, Todd. *The Word of God for the People of God: An Entryway to the Theological Interpretation of Scripture.* Grand Rapids: Eerdmans, 2010.

Boersma, Hans. *Violence, Hospitality, and the Cross: Reappropriating the Atonement Tradition.* Grand Rapids: Baker Academic, 2004.

Bonhoeffer, Dietrich. *Letters and Papers from Prison.* Edited by Eberhard Bethge. New York: Touchstone, 1997.

Bowens, Lisa M. *African American Readings of Paul: Reception, Resistance, and Transformation.* Grand Rapids: Eerdmans, 2020.

Bradshaw, Paul. "Difficulties in Doing Liturgical Theology." *Pacifica* 11, no. 2 (1998): 181–94.

Brown, Frank Burch. *Religious Aesthetics.* Princeton: Princeton University Press, 1993.

Brueggemann, Walter. *The Prophetic Imagination.* 40th anniversary ed. Minneapolis: Fortress, 2018.

———. "A Shape for Old Testament Theology, II: Embrace of Pain." *Catholic Biblical Quarterly* 47, no. 3 (1985): 395–415.

Burton, Tara Isabella. *Strange Rites: New Religions for a Godless World.* New York: PublicAffairs, 2020.

Callaway, Kutter, and Dean Batali. *Watching TV Religiously: Television and Theology in Dialogue.* Grand Rapids: Baker Academic, 2016.

Calvin, John. *Institutes of the Christian Religion.* Edited by John T. McNeill. Translated by Ford Lewis Battles. Louisville: Westminster John Knox, 2001.

Carnes, Natalie. "Breaking the Power of Monuments." *Stanford University Press Blog.* August 29, 2017. https://stanfordpress.typepad.com/blog/2017/08/breaking-the-power-of-monuments.html.

———. *Image and Presence: A Christological Reflection on Iconoclasm and Iconophilia.* Stanford, CA: Stanford University Press, 2017.

Carson, D. A. *The Gospel according to John.* Grand Rapids: Eerdmans, 1990.

Charles, Mark, and Soong-Chan Rah. *Unsettling Truths: The Ongoing, Dehumanizing Legacy of the Doctrine of Discovery.* Downers Grove, IL: InterVarsity, 2019.

Chesterton, G. K. "Our Note Book." *Illustrated London News,* 1928.

Clouser, Roy A. *The Myth of Religious Neutrality: An Essay on the Hidden Role of Religious Belief in Theories.* Notre Dame, IN: University of Notre Dame Press, 2005.

Coakley, Sarah. *God, Sexuality and the Self: An Essay "On the Trinity."* Cambridge: Cambridge University Press, 2013.

Cobb, Kelton. *The Blackwell Guide to Theology and Popular Culture.* Malden, MA: Blackwell, 2005.

Coen, Joel, and Ethan Coen, dirs. *The Big Lebowski.* United States: Gramercy Pictures, 1998.

Coles, Robert. *The Call of Service: A Witness to Idealism.* Boston: Mariner Books, 1994.

Cronk, Lee. *That Complex Whole: Culture and the Evolution of Human Behavior.* Boulder, CO: Westview, 1999.

Crouch, Andy. *Playing God: Redeeming the Gift of Power.* Downers Grove, IL: InterVarsity, 2013.

———. "The Return of Shame." *Christianity Today,* March 10, 2015. https://www.christianitytoday.com/ct/2015/march/andy-crouch-gospel-in-age-of-public-shame.html.

Curry, Tommy J. "Saved by the Bell: Derrick Bell's Racial Realism as Peda-
gogy." *Philosophical Studies in Education* 39 (2008): 35–46.

Dawkins, Richard. *The Selfish Gene*. New York: Oxford University Press,
1976.

de Botton, Alain. *Religion for Atheists: A Non-believer's Guide to the Uses
of Religion*. New York: Vintage, 2013.

de Brès, Guido. "The Belgic Confession." In *Our Faith*, edited by Leonard J.
Vander Zee, 25–68. Grand Rapids: Faith Alive, 2013.

Delgado, Richard, and Jean Stefancic. *Critical Race Theory: An Introduction*. 3rd ed. New York: New York University Press, 2017.

Dias, Elizabeth. "'Christianity Will Have Power.'" *New York Times*, August 9, 2020. https://www.nytimes.com/2020/08/09/us/evangelicals-trump
-christianity.html.

Donald, Merlin. *A Mind So Rare: The Evolution of Human Consciousness*.
New York: Norton, 2001.

Donne, John. *Devotions upon Emergent Occasions and Death's Duel*. New
York: Vintage, 1999.

Driesenga, Jessica. "A Pearl and a Leaven: The Twofold Call of the Gospel."
In *The Church's Social Responsibility*, edited by Jordan J. Ballor and
Robert Joustra, 39–45. Grand Rapids: Christian's Library, 2015.

Dubin, Charles S., dir. *Rodgers & Hammerstein's Cinderella*. Culver City:
Columbia TriStar Home Entertainment, 2001.

Durkheim, Émile. *The Elementary Forms of Religious Life*. Translated by
Karen E. Fields. New York: Free Press, 1995.

Dutton, Denis. *The Art Instinct: Beauty, Pleasure, and Human Evolution*.
London: Bloomsbury, 2010.

———. "A Darwinian Theory of Beauty." TED video, 15:33. February
2010. https://www.ted.com/talks/denis_dutton_a_darwinian_theory
_of_beauty?language=en.

Dyrness, William. *The Facts on the Ground: A Wisdom Theology of Culture*.
Eugene, OR: Cascade Books, 2021.

———. *Poetic Theology: God and the Poetics of Everyday Life*. Grand
Rapids: Eerdmans, 2011.

Eagleton, Terry. *Why Marx Was Right*. New Haven: Yale University Press,
2018.

Edelstein, David, Alison Willmore, Bilge Ebiri, and Angelica Jade Bastién.
"Every Movie of the 2010s, Ranked." *Vulture* (blog), *New York Maga-*

zine, December 11, 2019. https://www.vulture.com/article/every-movie
-of-the-2010s-ranked-sort-of.html.

Edgar, William. *Created and Creating: A Biblical Theology of Culture.* Downers Grove, IL: IVP Academic, 2016.

Eglinton, James. "Let Every Tongue Confess: Language Diversity and Reformed Public Theology." In *Reformed Public Theology*, edited by Matthew Kaemingk, 35–46. Grand Rapids: Baker Academic, 2021.

Eliot, T. S. *Notes towards the Definition of Culture.* New York: Harcourt, Brace, 1949.

Elizondo, Virgilio P. *Galilean Journey: The Mexican-American Promise.* Maryknoll, NY: Orbis Books, 2000.

Elmer, Duane. *Cross-Cultural Servanthood: Serving the World in Christlike Humility.* Downers Grove, IL: InterVarsity, 2006.

Engels, Friedrich. *Ludwig Feuerbach and the End of Classical German Philosophy.* Peking: Foreign Language Press, 1976.

Epstein, Seymour. *Constructive Thinking: The Key to Emotional Intelligence.* Westport, CT: Praeger, 1998.

Esack, Farid. *On Being a Muslim: Finding a Religious Path in the World Today.* Oxford: Oneworld, 1999.

Forbes, Bruce David, and Jeffrey H. Mahan, eds. *Religion and Popular Culture in America.* Oakland: University of California Press, 2017.

Foucault, Michel. *The Foucault Reader.* Edited by Paul Rabinow. New York: Pantheon, 1984.

Friedman, Edwin H. *A Failure of Nerve: Leadership in the Age of the Quick Fix.* Rev. ed. New York: Church Publishing, 2017.

Fujimura, Makoto. *Art and Faith: A Theology of Making.* New Haven: Yale University Press, 2020.

Geertz, Clifford. *The Interpretation of Cultures: Selected Essays.* New York: Basic Books, 1973.

Gladwell, Malcolm. *Talking to Strangers: What We Should Know about the People We Don't Know.* New York: Confer Books, 2019.

Godwin, Michael. "Meme, Counter-Meme." *Wired*, October 1, 1994. https://www.wired.com/1994/10/godwin-if-2/.

Goudzwaard, Bob, and Craig G. Bartholomew. *Beyond the Modern Age: An Archaeology of Contemporary Culture.* Downers Grove, IL: IVP Academic, 2017.

Grahame, Kenneth. *The Annotated Wind in the Willows*. Edited by Annie Gauger. New York: Norton, 2009.

Gramsci, Antonio. "Audacia e Fede." *Avanti*, May 22, 1916. Reprinted in *Sotto la Mole: 1916–1929*. Turin: Einaudi, 1960.

———. *Selections from the Prison Notebooks*. Edited by Quintin Hoare and Geoffrey Nowell Smith. 1971. Reprint, London: International Publishers, 1989.

Green, Gene L., Stephen T. Pardue, and K. K. Yeo, eds. *Majority World Theology*. Downers Grove, IL: IVP Academic, 2020.

Grenz, Stanley J., and John R. Franke. *Beyond Foundationalism: Shaping Theology in a Postmodern Context*. Louisville: Westminster John Knox, 2001.

Gutiérrez, Gustavo. *A Theology of Liberation: History, Politics, and Salvation*. Translated by Caridad Inda and John Eagleson. Maryknoll, NY: Orbis Books, 1988.

Haidt, Jonathan. *The Righteous Mind: Why Good People Are Divided by Politics and Religion*. New York: Vintage, 2013.

Harding, Susan Friend. "Representing Fundamentalism: The Problem of the Repugnant Cultural Other." *Social Research* 58, no. 2 (Summer 1991): 373–93.

Hauerwas, Stanley. *The Hauerwas Reader*. Edited by John Berkman and Michael G. Cartwright. Durham, NC: Duke University Press, 2001.

Horkheimer, Max. *Critical Theory: Selected Essays*. Translated by Matthew O'Connell. New York: Continuum, 1999.

Huizinga, Johan. *Homo Ludens: A Study of the Play-Element in Culture*. Boston: Beacon, 1955.

Hume, David. *Of the Standard of Taste, and Other Essays*. Indianapolis: Bobbs-Merrill, 1965.

Hyde, Lewis. *The Gift: How the Creative Spirit Transforms the World*. New York: Vintage, 2019.

Jacobs, Alan. *How to Think: A Survival Guide for a World at Odds*. New York: Currency, 2017.

———. "Plurality and Unity." *Snakes and Ladders* (blog). July 21, 2020. https://blog.ayjay.org/plurality-and-unity/.

Jennings, Willie James. *The Christian Imagination: Theology and the Origins of Race*. New Haven: Yale University Press, 2010.

Johnston, Robert K. *God's Wider Presence: Reconsidering General Revelation*. Grand Rapids: Baker Academic, 2014.

Kahneman, Daniel. *Thinking, Fast and Slow*. New York: Farrar, Straus & Giroux, 2013.

King, Martin Luther, Jr. *Strength to Love*. Minneapolis: Fortress, 1981.

Klapwijk, Jacob. "Antithesis and Common Grace." In *Bringing into Captivity Every Thought*, edited by Sander Griffioen, Gerben Groenewoud, and Jacob Klapwijk, 123–42. Lanham, MD: University Press of America, 1992.

Koyzis, David T. *Political Visions and Illusions: A Survey and Christian Critique of Contemporary Ideologies*. 2nd ed. Downers Grove, IL: IVP Academic, 2019.

———. *We Answer to Another: Authority, Office, and the Image of God*. Eugene, OR: Wipf & Stock, 2014.

Kuyper, Abraham. *Lectures on Calvinism*. Grand Rapids: Eerdmans, 1999.

Langberg, Diane. *Redeeming Power: Understanding Authority and Abuse in the Church*. Grand Rapids: Brazos, 2020.

Lasseter, John, dir. *Toy Story*. United States: Buena Vista Pictures, 1995.

Lathrop, Gordon. *Holy Things: A Liturgical Theology*. Minneapolis: Fortress, 1993.

Lee, Li Young. "From Blossoms." In *Joy: 100 Poems*, edited by Christian Wiman, 54. New Haven: Yale University Press, 2017.

Lewis, C. S. *Mere Christianity*. New York: HarperCollins, 2009.

———. *The Screwtape Letters*. New York: HarperOne, 2015.

———. *The Silver Chair*. New York: HarperCollins, 2002.

———. *The Weight of Glory*. New York: Macmillan, 1949.

Lindbeck, George A. *The Nature of Doctrine: Religion and Theology in a Postliberal Age*. Philadelphia: Westminster, 1984.

Liou, Jeff. "Critical Race Theory, Campus Culture, and the Reformed Tradition." In *Reformed Public Theology*, edited by Matthew Kaemingk, 237–50. Grand Rapids: Baker Academic, 2021.

Loconte, Joseph. *A Hobbit, a Wardrobe, and a Great War: How J. R. R. Tolkien and C. S. Lewis Rediscovered Faith, Friendship, and Heroism in the Cataclysm of 1914–1918*. Nashville: Thomas Nelson, 2017.

Lovejoy, Arthur O. *The Great Chain of Being: A Study of the History of an Idea*. Cambridge, MA: Harvard University Press, 1976.

Luhrmann, T. M. *How God Becomes Real: Kindling the Presence of Invisible Others*. Princeton: Princeton University Press, 2020.

Lyden, John C., and Eric Michael Mazur, eds. *The Routledge Companion to Religion and Popular Culture*. London: Routledge, 2015.

MacDonald, George. *A Dish of Orts*. Whitethorn, CA: Johannesen, 1996.

———. *Unspoken Sermons: Series I, II, III in One Volume*. Whitethorn, CA: Johannesen, 1999.

MacIntyre, Alasdair. *After Virtue: A Study in Moral Theory*. 3rd ed. Notre Dame, IN: University of Notre Dame Press, 2007.

Marsh, Clive, and Gaye Ortiz, eds. *Explorations in Theology and Film: An Introduction*. Malden, MA: Wiley, 1997.

Martel, J. F. *Reclaiming Art in the Age of Artifice: A Treatise, Critique, and Call to Action*. Berkeley: North Atlantic Books, 2015.

Marx, Karl. *Selected Writings*. Edited by Lawrence H. Simon. Indianapolis: Hackett, 1994.

Marx, Karl, and Friedrich Engels. *The Communist Manifesto*. New York: Bantam, 1992.

McCaulley, Esau. "I Have Only One Hope for Racial Justice: A God Who Conquered Death." *Christianity Today*, June 10, 2020. https://www.christianitytoday.com/ct/2020/june-web-only/george-floyd-racial-justice-hope-god-who-conquered-death.html.

McLuhan, Marshall, and Quentin Fiore. *The Medium Is the Massage: An Inventory of Effects*. Corte Madera, CA: Gingko Press, 2001.

Milbank, John, Graham Ward, and Edith Wyschogrod. *Theological Perspectives on God and Beauty*. Harrisburg, PA: Trinity Press International, 2003.

Morales, L. Michael. *Who Shall Ascend the Mountain of the Lord? A Biblical Theology of the Book of Leviticus*. New Studies in Biblical Theology. Downers Grove, IL: IVP Academic, 2015.

Mouw, Richard J. *Abraham Kuyper: A Short and Personal Introduction*. Grand Rapids: Eerdmans, 2011.

———. *Uncommon Decency: Christian Civility in an Uncivil World*. Downers Grove, IL: InterVarsity, 2010.

Muck, Terry C. *Why Study Religion? Understanding Humanity's Pursuit of the Divine*. Grand Rapids: Baker Academic, 2016.

Netland, Harold. *Encountering Religious Pluralism: The Challenge to Christian Faith and Mission*. Downers Grove, IL: InterVarsity, 2001.

Niebuhr, H. Richard. *Christ and Culture*. San Francisco: Harper & Row, 1975.

Noll, Mark A. *The Civil War as a Theological Crisis*. Durham: University of North Carolina Press, 2006.

Otto, Rudolf. *The Idea of the Holy*. New York: Oxford University Press, 1958.

Parker, Kim, Rachel Minkin, and Jesse Bennett. "Economic Fallout from COVID-19 Continues to Hit Lower-Income Americans the Hardest." Pew Research Center, September 24, 2020. https://www.pewresearch.org /social-trends/2020/09/24/economic-fallout-from-covid-19-continues-to -hit-lower-income-americans-the-hardest/.

Parsons, William B., ed. *Being Spiritual but Not Religious: Past, Present, Future(s)*. Milton Park, UK: Routledge, 2020.

Pieper, Josef. *Leisure: The Basis of Culture*. Translated by James V. Schall. San Francisco: Ignatius, 2009.

Plantinga, Alvin. *Where the Conflict Really Lies: Science, Religion, and Naturalism*. New York: Oxford University Press, 2011.

Plantinga, Cornelius, Jr. *Not the Way It's Supposed to Be: A Breviary of Sin*. Grand Rapids: Eerdmans, 1996.

Plato. *The Dialogues of Plato*. Vol. 2, *The Symposium*, translated by R. E. Allen. New Haven: Yale University Press, 1993.

———. *The Republic of Plato*. Translated by Allan Bloom. New York: Basic Books, 2016.

Pohl, Christine D. *Making Room: Recovering Hospitality as a Christian Tradition*. Grand Rapids: Eerdmans, 1999.

Rawls, John. *A Theory of Justice*. Cambridge, MA: Harvard University Press, 1999.

Red Carpet News TV. "Bill Murray Admits a Painting Saved His Life." You-Tube video, 2:40. February 11, 2014. https://www.youtube.com/watch?v =8eOIcWB7jSA.

Richter, Sandra L. *The Epic of Eden: A Christian Entry into the Old Testament*. Downers Grove, IL: IVP Academic, 2008.

Rilke, Rainer Maria. "Archaic Torso of Apollo." Academy of American Poets. Accessed November 22, 2020. https://poets.org/poem/archaic-torso-apollo.

Robinson, Marilynne. *Absence of Mind: The Dispelling of Inwardness from the Modern Myth of the Self*. New Haven: Yale University Press, 2011.

———. *Housekeeping*. New York: Picador, 1980.

———. *What Are We Doing Here? Essays*. New York: Farrar, Straus & Giroux, 2018.

Rookmaaker, Hans. *The Creative Gift: Essays on Art and Christian Living*. Westchester, IL: Cornerstone Books, 1981.

Rothstein, Richard. *The Color of Law: A Forgotten History of How Our Government Segregated America*. New York: Liveright, 2017.

Ryken, Leland, James C. Wilhoit, and Tremper Longman III, eds. *Dictionary of Biblical Imagery*. Downers Grove, IL: InterVarsity, 2010.

Sandel, Michael J. *Justice: What's the Right Thing to Do?* New York: Farrar, Straus & Giroux, 2010.

Sanneh, Lamin. *Translating the Message: The Missionary Impact on Culture*. Maryknoll, NY: Orbis Books, 2009.

Schleiermacher, Friedrich. *On Religion: Speeches to Its Cultured Despisers*. Translated by John Oman. New York: Harper & Row, 1958.

Seerveld, Calvin. *Rainbows for the Fallen World: Aesthetic Life and Artistic Task*. Toronto: Tuppence, 1980.

Skillen, James W. *God's Sabbath with Creation: Vocations Fulfilled, the Glory Unveiled*. Eugene, OR: Wipf & Stock, 2019.

Sloterdijk, Peter. *Bubbles*. Vol. 1 of *Spheres: Microspherology*. Los Angeles: Semiotext(e), 2011.

Smedes, Lewis B. *My God and I: A Spiritual Memoir*. Grand Rapids: Eerdmans, 2003.

Smith, Christian. *The Bible Made Impossible: Why Biblicism Is Not a Truly Evangelical Reading of Scripture*. Grand Rapids: Brazos, 2012.

Smith, Christian, with Melinda Lundquist Denton. *Soul Searching: The Religious and Spiritual Lives of American Teenagers*. Oxford: Oxford University Press, 2005.

Smith, James K. A. *Desiring the Kingdom: Worship, Worldview, and Cultural Formation*. Grand Rapids: Baker Academic, 2009.

———. *Imagining the Kingdom: How Worship Works*. Grand Rapids: Baker Academic, 2013.

———. *You Are What You Love: The Spiritual Power of Habit*. Grand Rapids, MI: Brazos, 2016.

Smith, Jason E. *Religious but Not Religious: Living a Symbolic Life*. Asheville, NC: Chiron, 2020.

Smith, Robert S. "Cultural Marxism: Imaginary Conspiracy or Revolutionary Reality?" *Themelios* 44, no. 3 (2019): 436–65.

Smith, Wilfred Cantwell. *The Meaning and End of Religion*. New York: Harper & Row, 1962.

Stassen, Glen. *Authentic Transformation: A New Vision of Christ and Culture*. Nashville: Abingdon, 1995.

Stazler, Wendy, dir. *Parks and Recreation*. 2011. Season 3, episode 2, "Flu Season." Aired January 27, 2011, on NBC.

Swinburne, A. C. "The Garden of Proserpine." Poetry Foundation. Accessed April 10, 2021. https://www.poetryfoundation.org/poems/45288/the-garden-of-proserpine.

Tanner, Kathryn. *Theories of Culture: A New Agenda for Theology*. Minneapolis: Fortress, 1997.

Tatarkiewicz, Wladyslaw. "The Great Theory of Beauty and Its Decline." *Journal of Aesthetics and Art Criticism* 31, no. 2 (1972): 165–80.

Taylor, Charles. *A Secular Age*. Cambridge, MA: Harvard University Press, 2007.

———. *Sources of the Self: The Making of the Modern Identity*. Cambridge, MA: Harvard University Press, 1992.

ter Kuile, Casper, and Angie Thurston. "How We Gather." April 18, 2015. https://caspertk.files.wordpress.com/2015/04/how-we-gather.pdf.

Tillich, Paul. *Theology of Culture*. New York: Oxford University Press, 1959.

Tisby, Jemar. *How to Fight Racism: Courageous Christianity and the Journey toward Racial Justice*. Grand Rapids: Zondervan, 2021.

Tolkien, J. R. R. *The Letters of J. R. R. Tolkien*. Boston: Houghton Mifflin, 1981.

———. *The Return of the King*. Boston: Houghton Mifflin, 1965.

———. *Tree and Leaf*. Boston: Houghton Mifflin, 1965.

———. *The Two Towers*. Boston: Houghton Mifflin, 1965.

Tracy, David. *The Analogical Imagination: Christian Theology and the Culture of Pluralism*. New York: Crossroad, 1998.

———. *Blessed Rage for Order: The New Pluralism in Theology*. Chicago: University of Chicago Press, 1996.

United States Conference of Catholic Bishops. "Option for the Poor and Vulnerable." Accessed August 17, 2021. https://www.usccb.org/beliefs-and-teachings/what-we-believe/catholic-social-teaching/option-for-the-poor-and-vulnerable.

Vanhoozer, Kevin J. *The Drama of Doctrine: A Canonical-Linguistic Approach to Christian Theology*. Louisville: Westminster John Knox, 2005.

———. *Remythologizing Theology: Divine Action, Passion, and Authorship*. Cambridge Studies in Christian Doctrine. Cambridge: Cambridge University Press, 2010.

Vanhoozer, Kevin J., Charles A. Anderson, and Michael Sleasman, eds. *Everyday Theology: How to Read Cultural Texts and Interpret Trends.* Grand Rapids: Baker Academic, 2007.

Visser, Paul J. *Heart for the Gospel, Heart for the World.* Eugene, OR: Wipf & Stock, 2003.

Volf, Miroslav. *Exclusion and Embrace: A Theological Exploration of Identity, Otherness, and Reconciliation.* Rev. ed. Nashville: Abingdon, 2019.

Volf, Miroslav, and Ryan McAnnally-Linz. *Public Faith in Action: How to Engage with Commitment, Conviction, and Courage.* Grand Rapids: Brazos, 2017.

Wallace, David Foster. *This Is Water: Some Thoughts, Delivered on a Significant Occasion, about Living a Compassionate Life.* New York: Little, Brown, 2009.

Walls, Andrew. *The Missionary Movement in Christian History: Studies in the Transmission of Faith.* Maryknoll, NY: Orbis Books, 1996.

Winner, Lauren F. *The Dangers of Christian Practice: On Wayward Gifts, Characteristic Damage, and Sin.* New Haven: Yale University Press, 2018.

Wolfe, Judith. "The Relevance of Theology in the University and Society Today." University of St. Andrews. YouTube video, 24:54. March 29, 2021. https://www.youtube.com/watch?v=FMtnHG3Y9aE&ab_channel =UniversityofStAndrews.

Wolterstorff, Nicholas. *In This World of Wonders: Memoir of a Life in Learning.* Grand Rapids: Eerdmans, 2019.

———. *Journey toward Justice: Personal Encounters in The Global South.* Grand Rapids: Baker Academic, 2013.

———. *Justice: Rights and Wrongs.* Princeton: Princeton University Press, 2010.

Zahl, David. *Seculosity: How Career, Parenting, Technology, Food, Politics, and Romance Became Our New Religion and What to Do about It.* Minneapolis: Fortress, 2019.

Žižek, Slavoj. "If There Is a God, Then Anything Is Permitted." ABC (Australian Broadcasting Corporation) Religion & Ethics, April 17, 2012. https://www.abc.net.au/religion/if-there-is-a-god-then-anything-is-permitted /10100616.

SCRIPTURE INDEX